SIMENON IN COURT

By the same Author

ENGLAND'S ON THE ANVIL
THE DOGE OF DOVER

Edited by John Raymond

THE BALDWIN AGE
THE LETTERS OF QUEEN VICTORIA
THE MEMOIRS OF CAPTAIN GRONOW

JOHN RAYMOND

Simenon in Court

HAMISH HAMILTON
LONDON

First published in Great Britain, 1968
by Hamish Hamilton Ltd.,
90 Great Russell Street, London W.C.1
Copyright © 1968 by John Raymond

SBN 241 01505 7 7907

Frontispieçe photograph by Jerry Bauer

MADE AND PRINTED IN GREAT BRITAIN BY
MORRISON AND GIBB LIMITED, LONDON AND EDINBURGH

To Mary

Contents

Prefatory Note

MY thanks are due to friends who have been good enough to read this book, or parts of it, in manuscript, and have contributed valuable suggestions, by which I greatly profited; in particular to Pamela Hansford Johnson and Stephen Constant. I am further much indebted to Philip Hope-Wallace and Ronald Payne for advice on many points raised in the text; to my patient publishers and particularly to Christopher Sinclair-Stevenson (whose interest in Simenon transcends the professional); and to Pamela Wadsworth, who typed the manuscript so unerringly. I owe the greatest debt of all to my friend the late Peter Duval Smith, who first prompted and then encouraged me to write the book.

Readers of Bernard de Fallois's invaluable introduction to Simenon's fiction will be aware of how much the present study has gained from his analysis. My grateful acknowledgements are due to Miss Brigid Brophy and Messrs. Jonathan Cape for permission to quote from *Don't Never Forget*; to Messrs. Secker and Warburg for the quotation from the late Justin O'Brien's translation of the *Journals* of André Gide; and to Messrs. Routledge and Hamish Hamilton for permission to make use of excerpts from their standard copyright translations.

J.R.

Introduction

IN his excellent and ultra-discriminatory study of the French novel, Martin Turnell remarks on how he once said to a Frenchman, 'I wish someone would explain to me what the French see in Balzac.' 'I read him,' the Frenchman replied, 'as I read Simenon.' For Turnell, exasperated by Balzac's 'limited' intelligence and 'crude' sensibility, his 'highly personal' melodrama and interests 'by no means those of an adult', the explanation is all-sufficing. If the author of *La Rabouilleuse* may be said to have inaugurated the *roman policier*, the novels of Georges Simenon, or at least a large number of them, are the end-product of this type of fiction. If Simenon's preoccupations are quite different from Balzac's, and his world not entirely similar to Balzac's 'world of crime and fraud, a world where the Swindler and the Strumpet are supreme', it is true that 'he often succeeds . . . by the story-teller's gift of making us want to know "what happens next" '. Both Balzac and Simenon may be charged with creating 'the illusion that we enjoy "literature" when we are really responding at a much lower level or, to put it in another way, in much of his work Balzac raises the detective story and the *roman d'aventure* to the level of a sort of art'. That this 'sort of art' is an outstanding one, and the Frenchman's comparison by no means as backhanded a compliment as Turnell would have us imagine, is the basic contention and purpose of this book.

Georges Simenon is not only the greatest story-teller of our day. He is—to put the matter in blunt, critical shorthand—an eighth type of literary ambiguity. His range, versatility and sheer production baffle his addicts and enrage his critics. Part poet and part journalist, part showman and part shaman, he is among the supreme craftsmen of the art of fiction, its contemporary Pied Piper, one who has created a whole *discothèque* of disturbing dreams under the hill. Each of his seasoned listeners begins a new melodic line with the sinking certainty that the music will gradually but inevitably draw him into some original and sinister cave of the imagination. 'God knows,' he murmurs, as he turns Page One, 'into what heart of darkness he is going to lead us now!'

At his best, because he sounds this very note of uncertainty—man's uncertainty of himself and of his relationship to others—Simenon is the most significant and the least difficult writer of our time. In the works of the majority of great novelists over the last two hundred years, the moral message, however complex, comes to us loudly and clearly enough. We all know where we stand in relation to Dorothea in *Middlemarch* or to Gertrude in *Daniel Deronda*. Henry James, for all his nuances and subtle shading, is morally as clean as a whistle. (The fact that the ethic gets severely twisted on occasion is beside the point; James's own attitude to his creatures is always beautifully lucid.) Proust in his way judges as firmly as Lawrence in his, Joyce Cary maintains Protestant values, or stands them on their head, as devotedly as Graham Greene deploys his highly individual scheme of Catholic salvation. But Simenon, for the most part, refuses to judge. He is content to present—and leave it at that.

It is chiefly for this reason that none of his readers sees his work in quite the same way, just as none of us dream the same nightmares. Hence the diversity of opinions, the enthusiasm and antipathy, the violent reactions that his work arouses on all sides and at many levels. For Simenon has not only slain his tens of thousands of readers; his fellow-artists—Gide, Colette, Mauriac, Eliot, Cocteau, Max Jacob, Maugham, Céline—have all owned to his widdershins power.

'Some people collect stamps,' he told M. Albert Parinaud, 'I collect human beings.' During his forty-odd years as a writer, Simenon has certainly collected a volume of critical opinion around his fiction. Thus, for M. Parinaud—whose portentous three-volume study (*Connaissance de Georges Simenon*) has still to be completed—almost everything in his work stems from and has its source in his childhood and is to be found in his long, semi-autobiographical novel, *Pedigree*. For M. Gilbert Sigaux, on the other hand—and the present writer agrees with him—this is a gross over-simplification. There are writers—Alain-Fournier, the author of *Le Grand Meaulnes*, is a case in point—whose genius is rooted in childhood and adolescence, but Simenon is not one of them. Incidentally, M. Sigaux has adduced a powerful and ingenious argument for Simenon's refusal to pass moral judgment or to resolve his characters' feelings and motivation in terms of any current psychological system, merely posing their problems and situations, following them through and allowing their destinies to hang in mid-air without comment. Such a silence on the writer's part, or 'elision' as he terms it, does not mean that Simenon has shirked or skirted his creative responsibilities, but rather that in the present and limited state of our knowledge of the human psyche, he believes that they are better left undiscussed.

For 'Conrad Rietzlen', whose study *Simenon, Avocat des Hommes* is the most genuine and eloquent witness to his art that has yet been written (the fact that the pseudonym conceals the identity of a well-known Paris doctor must please the subject of his book immensely), Simenon is leading counsel for humanity, a writer who holds a dock brief for the world and believes, like the late C. S. Lewis but for quite other reasons, that 'there are no *ordinary* men and women'. For Anne Richter, whose *Georges Simenon et l'Homme Désintégré*, though diffuse and existentially metaphysical, is full of interest, he is the restorer of Everyman's twentieth-century image. The man-in-the-street, whose identity, damaged by the erosion of those old breakwaters, class and religion, has been finally sapped by Kafka, Pirandello, Beckett, Artaud, Michaux and (save the mark!) Françoise Sagan, must be rebuilt on a new model. This, Mlle Richter suggests, is the herculean task that Simenon is now performing for the human imagination. M. Thomas Narcejac, whose study (*Le Cas Simenon*) contains numerous insights, goes almost as far when he declares that 'Simenon is trying to show us how man may be renewed. He is the novelist of a new beginning'. For Charles Plisnier, who takes his stand, as do many Simenonians, on *Le Testament Donadieu*, he is the supremely credible romantic. For Roger Nimier he is Gogol's direct descendant, for Marcel Aymé, 'Balzac without the *longueurs*'.

All these opinions are relevant to Simenon's art yet all fall short of defining its nature for, to be truthful, it is almost impossible to contain his works in a formula. Pass almost any broad judgment on his work, make any generalization you please, and you are at once brought up short by contradictory evidence. If I know this, it is by painful experience. Time and again in preparing this study and noting down apparent general clues about Simenon's fiction, I have been confronted by an exception that seems to prove the rule, only to have that exception bolstered and fortified by yet another instance and then another. In this way the elusive Simenon, a hind let loose, slips from the reader's tether and is away.

A single example shall suffice. After reading a good number of his novels, I had reached the conclusion that the women in Simenon's fiction, however dramatic and important the roles assigned them, were really adjuncts, accessories before the fact, agents rather than patients. They might be said to act upon his heroes, they were often the cause of the men's self-destructive destinies, they gave them their *coup de grâce*. Thus Tamatéa is the cause of Oscar Donadieu's suicide, Claire is the victim of Avaloine's act of passion, the desire to kill his wife obsesses M. Émile of *Dimanche*. All the Little Man from Archangel's miseries are set in motion by his wife's disappearance, Yvette in *En cas de malheur* is largely there to create that strangely Camus-like hero, the infatuated Maître Gobillot. It was the same in the Maigret series—from *Pietr-le-Letton* onwards it was the women who were the spurs and the victims, the temptresses and the whippers-in. Having worked this all out, as I thought very neatly, I began re-reading *Le Testament Donadieu*—one of Simenon's central and most impressive works, which I had deliberately set aside for a late stage of the exploration. Instantly, the whole theoretical house of cards collapsed. It is Martine, the awakening and at last awakened wife of Philippe Dargens, who is the turning centre of the book—a genuine Stendhalian heroine after the model of Elizabeth in *Le Rouge et le Noir*. Philippe himself is the merest cardboard Julien Sorel by comparison. The outstanding case of Martine pointed the way to a dozen instances where the women in Simenon's novels were uppermost. Few of his gallery of women portraits are as grimly painted as Madame Bauve in *Le Haut Mal*, none is as memorable as the mother in *Le Petit Saint*. As for Maigret's chamber of horrors, it was, when one reviewed the matter, a veritable Hecate's wardrobe of villainesses—from that sinister and charming old lady in Etretat (*Maigret et la Vieille Dame*), through the terrible and tigerish Aline (*Maigret se défend* and *La Patience de Maigret*) to the old vulturess of *Signé Picpus*.

That, plainly and simply, is the difficulty of writing about Simenon. Once you have looked at his art in the round, it is extremely hard to define or to contain it—the more so, since he is in the full vigour of his creative life and has, in the past five years, written three novels as remarkable, in an entirely new way, as anything he has produced previously. In the chapter that follows, therefore, in place of the biographical outline that is customary at the beginning of a study of this kind, I have tried to set down a few of the most blatant contradictions and paradoxes in Simenon's work that confront the reader at the outset. This book, since it is about a living writer whose achievement is by no means yet complete, must in its nature be an interim account— a dossier of the kind that Maigret's *juge d'instruction* assembles for the Parquet before the Public Prosecutor can act. The pages that immediately follow, therefore, are merely submitted as evidence that *Le cas Simenon* is a highly complicated case.

Chapter 1

KNOCKESPOTCH

How to describe a prodigy—a creative achievement still in process? At the age of sixty-five, Georges Simenon is not only creating works of art, but he is still evolving and powerfully changing his shape as a writer. Such a case is without parallel in contemporary literature. It is not simply a question of the sheer number of books he has piled up behind him. In terms of the variety of atmospheres and ambiances he has explored, the countless changes of scene that he has shifted, the different methods and tempos he employs and the vast repertory of characters he has created, Simenon remains an amazement, almost an enormity. He can only, so it seems, be explained by comparison. Hence the inky thumbs pointed knowingly backwards towards Balzac—an obvious but a highly misleading reference-point which will need a good deal of discussion later in this book. At the outset we are reduced to allegory, and here Dr. Lemprière is of assistance. Proteus, so his dictionary tells us, was a sea-deity, the son of Oceanus and Tethys. 'He usually resided in the Carpathian Sea and like the rest of the gods, reposed himself on the sea shore, where such as wished to consult him, generally resorted; he was difficult of access, and when consulted, refused to give answers, by assuming different shapes and eluding the grasp.'

An assumer of infinite shapes, a refuser of life's answers. The cap fits Simenon exactly—except that, as the millions of readers who devour his books have long ago demonstrated, he is by no means difficult of access. Writing some six years ago, M. Roger Stéphane estimated that with an average of six novels being published every twelve months in some thirty languages, a new Simenon made its appearance somewhere in the world every third day. Since 1929, Simenon has written some two hundred works of fiction under his own name. Previously, partly to free himself from journalism, partly and quite deliberately to prepare himself for his vocation as a writer, he produced, under one or another of his sixteen pseudonyms (including the original 'Sim') countless specimens of what he now calls 'my pulp fiction'; all this beside short stories and articles. These vilely printed and garishly illustrated twopence-coloureds are now rare collector's items. The titles—*Le Gorille-Roi*, *Le Chinois de San Francisco*, *L'Ile des Maudits*, *Le Yacht Fantôme*, *Katia Acrobate*, etc.—speak for themselves. One is reminded of Mr. Cardan's description in Huxley's *Crome Yellow* of the tales of Knockespotch: 'Oh those Tales! Those Tales! How shall I describe them? Fabulous characters shoot across his pages like gaily dressed performers on the trapeze. There are extraordinary adventures and still more extraordinary speculations. Intelligences and emotions, relieved of all the imbecile promptings of civilized life, move in intricate and subtle dances crossing and re-crossing, advancing, retiring, impinging . . .' Far from being repentant about his juvenilia, Simenon displays them proudly to the visitor alongside his mature work in the foursquare bookroom in which he houses his entire published writings. They are his diploma, proof of a successful apprenticeship to his craft. Craft, not art, be it noted, for it is as a craftsman, he insists, that he wishes to be judged. To achieve brevity and precision, to pare away every trace of the inessential and the superfluous, Simenon maintains that he was forced to follow this road. It is not, he would agree, a recipe for every writer's case. Yet however generally uncritical of, because genuinely uninterested in, the art of most other writers—the sharp exceptions to this generalization will be considered in their place—he still implies that a number of his more squeamish fellow-craftsmen might benefit from the discipline of a pulp apprenticeship.

An assumer of shapes. No writer in this century has created such a volume of human character as Simenon. In this at least his achievement can be legitimately matched with Balzac's. Yet here the critic comes up against Paradox One. On paper, given time, application and a substantial research grant from an American university, it would be possible to construct a biographical dictionary of Simenonian characters analogous to the two-volume repertoire of Balzac's *Comédie Humaine*. Gautier estimated Balzac's personae at a round two thousand. In the course of my own reading of something like a half of Simenon's fiction, I have jotted down a list of roughly one thousand men, women and children (excluding concierges, garage mechanics, gendarmes, criminal pick-ups, peasants, hotel staff and similar grades and extras) whose fictional identities are sufficiently individual and personified to merit inclusion in such a volume. Yet whereas Balzac, concerned to construct a whole linked sociology of human beings, would glory in such a tribute to his creative prowess, Simenon would not be flattered to be told that such a project was in train. For Simenon, theoretically concerned as he is with men and women in the solitude of their individual destinies, the human social surround is merely so much over-spill. As he has declared again and again, in press interviews, on television and elsewhere, it is with man, man naked and without his attributes, that he is concerned.

But this is only one aspect of the Simenon paradox. There are a heap of others. Thus it could be said, in a spirit of legitimate exasperation, that our whole understanding of his art is complicated, vitiated even, at the start by the image of himself as writer that this Proteus of the moral situation has chosen to impose upon his public. Here you have an artist of genius who, while disclaiming any interest in whole acres of human affairs and large categories of the human tragi-comedy—everything and everybody, that is to say, concerned with war, religion, politics, big business, every form of officialdom and bureaucracy—yet reveals, at every turn in his work and by unconscious sleight of hand, that he has a unique, intuitive knowledge of all these ways of life, religion only excepted. ('You will find no priests in my fiction!' he boasted to me triumphantly. Yet even in this department, he displays on occasion a clinical knowledge of institutionalized Christianity of which only an ex-prize pupil of the Society of Jesus, himself once destined for the priesthood, might be deemed capable.)

And there are all the other paradoxes of Simenon—including the extraordinary contradictions of his style, a style in which, as Raymond Mortimer has well described it, 'clichés remain side by side with brilliant images, so that the style presents a model not of elegance but economy' and hence 'the resulting works appear more akin to films at their best than any previous novels'. This ability to combine the excitement of a good film with the realization of character in depth is an original mark of Simenon's fiction, and partly owes its success to his development of the fictional flashback. Yet it remains a paradox that such a stream-lined writer should at the same time be one of the most poetic of living novelists, a stylist who by no means always prefers the *mot moyen* to the *mot juste*.

Again, take the contradiction of Simenon as scene-shifter. Whether he writes of Tahiti or Montparnasse, café society in Istanbul (*Les Clients d'Avrenos*) or the hermitages of the Galapagos, the luxury of the Hôtel Georges Cinq or the tenements of Batum, Breton farmsteads, pauper shelters in Warsaw, the Negro quarter of Panama or the first-, second- and third-class decks of the Messageries Maritimes, this connoisseur of environment with his genius for localizing the universal in the particular, displays a horror of admitting to immediate influences. Indeed, he tells you, he has been in all these places—long ago, often years before he wrote the novel in which he has captured their atmospheres so impressively. Simenon has never been a note-taker; he is no researcher or paymaster of others' researches. Like most great novelists, he is concerned to mediate his experience, first through memory, then through imagination. Only in the case of *Pedigree*, that tour-de-force of semi-autobiography, is the metamorphosis absent.

In the case of live or dead human-beings whose *traits et gestes* have served or contributed in some way to the formation of one or other of his characters, Simenon, in conversation the most equable and forthcoming of men, becomes mildly bristly. At first sight, from a purely practical standpoint, this is understandable. One remembers the spate of libel actions brought by the outraged Liègeois that attended the original version of *Pedigree*—*Je me souviens*, a more direct, unciphered version of the writer's childhood and adolescence. There was also the case of the hotel proprietress at Libreville in Gabon who sued Simenon successfully after the publication of *Le Coup de Lune*. Such episodes teach the writer to take precautions. Again, there is the artist's legitimate pride, his refusal to allow that the genuine creation of his brain should be dismissed merely as a caricature or pastiche of real life. The allegation that Tom Driffield in *Cakes and Ale* *must* be either Meredith or Thomas Hardy or a mixture of both—when anyone with the slightest knowledge of either could see that the old hoodwinker in Maugham's book was nothing of the kind—caused its author much urbane chagrin. (True, Alroy Kear in the same book *was* Hugh Walpole, but since he was still alive and supposedly a friend of Maugham's, and was known to have practically swooned on opening the book, the portrait had necessarily to be disclaimed.)

It is in the Driffield sense that Simenon declares, in a foreword to *Les Volets Verts* (1950), that his study of a great comedian (Maugin) is in no sense a *roman à clef*—no veiled portrait of Raimu, Michel Simon, W. C. Fields or Charlie Chaplin ('whom I consider the great actors of our time') is intended, however much the writer may have borrowed certain professional traits to raise his hero to their stature. 'The rest is pure fiction, my hero's character, his background, his childhood, the episodes of his career, his public or private life, his death. Maugin *n'est ni Untel ni Untel, c'est Maugin* . . .' It is a robust, Balzacian affirmation. Though, indeed, it is hard to imagine the down-to-earth Simenon calling on Maugin's doctor, the great diagnostician Biguet, in the same way as Balzac cried on his deathbed, 'Send for Bianchon! Only Bianchon can save me now!'

On the other hand, take *Le Président*, that terse, impressionistic sketch of past greatness turned futile, but never senile, by invalid old age. There he sits, the ex-Prime Minister of France, in the Louis-Philippe armchair 'that he had lugged round with him from one Ministry to another for forty years, till it had become a legend', waiting impatiently for news of a government crisis on the five o'clock radio bulletin:

> As the years went by his skin had grown thinner and smoother, with white blotches that gave it the appearance of marble, and by now it clung to the prominent cheek-bones and sheathed his skeleton so closely that his features, as they became more strongly marked, seemed to be gradually fining down. In the village once he had heard one little boy call out to another: 'Look at that old death's-head!'

He sat without stirring, scarcely a yard away from the log fire, whose flames crackled now and then in a sudden down-draught, his hands folded on his stomach in the position in which they would be placed when his dead body was laid out. Would anybody have the nerve, then, to slip a rosary between his fingers, as someone had done to one of his colleagues, who'd also been several times Prime Minister and a leading Freemason?

Once prepotent, the ex-Prime Minister is a national institution in grand decay, tended by the nurse and doctors he detests, shielded by the devoted secretary he despises, guarded by plain-clothes policemen. Raging and fuming in his chair, he prowls and paces to and fro in memory, a crabby old tiger of distinction caged in a provincial zoo. And, of course, Simenon's Président is the Tiger himself, the spitting image of Clemenceau in retirement. Having read and admired the novel, I re-read Hampden Jackson's excellent study of the statesman on whose resentful and bitter old age the book seemed based. It is all there (I quote from Jackson), 'his realism, his logic and his wit, his distrustfulness and malice . . . the very paradoxes of his character—in which contempt was combined with kindness, cruelty with pity, frivolity with moral purpose, individualism with patriotism . . .' As if this were not enough, there are the factual similarities. Like Clemenceau, Simenon's great man has been cheated of the Presidency of the Republic. (Clemenceau's supplanter, the foppish Deschanel, retired to a mental home shortly after his election. Here, even Simenon has not attempted to improve on history!) Like Clemenceau, his published memoirs bear no relation to the book he could have written, and which, in the case of Simenon's states-man, he is secretly rewriting, scattering his hair-raising and incriminatory revelations between the leaves of Saint-Simon's memoirs and other favourite volumes in his library. Like Clem-enceau, he has been reviled by the Left for using troops as strike-breakers. Like Clemenceau, he has more than once saved his country, he is the man France sends for when everyone else has failed, the man who believes, like the Tiger, that 'democracy is the art of disciplining oneself'. Who else could this be—Briand, Poincaré, Millerand, Blum?—but Georges Benjamin Clemenceau to the life?

Yet when, in conversation at Epalinges, I put this question

of basic identity to Simenon, he pooh-poohed the suggestion. No, he had not been thinking of Clemenceau at all! He had never had the statesman in his mind. Why this seeming denial of Peter?

I have cited this instance at length because it seems to shed light from a number of angles on much that appears contradictory in Simenon's fiction—and indeed, in his own attitude toward his genius. Confronted with Simenon's basic situation, Balzac would have rubbed his hands with excitement. Submerged in history, in all the personalities, circumstances and trappings engendered by Napoleon, he was in himself, as his worshipper Barbey d'Aurevilly remarked, 'a literary Bonaparte who never had to abdicate or to lose the Battle of Waterloo'. As such, the plot of *Le Président* would have appealed to him immensely.

The ministry has fallen and the ex-Premier's one-time secretary, Chalamont, has been asked to form a government. But Chalamont has once, long ago, betrayed both the Premier and his country. The Premier still holds his written confession hidden away among the other documents in his library. A single telephone call and Chalamont's career will be *kaput*:

> There were at least ten numbers on the tip of his tongue, he knew them by heart, and he need only ring one of them in order to sink the ministry that was being formed.
>
> He was on the point of doing it, and the effort to contain himself, remain worthy of himself, was so great that he felt an attack coming on. His fingers, his knees began to shake, and as usual at such moments his nerves refused to obey him; the mechanism suddenly began to race at increasing speed.
>
> Without a word he went hastily into his bedroom, hoping Milleran had not noticed anything and wouldn't go and fetch Madame Blanche. With feverish haste he snatched out of a drawer two sedative pills, prescribed for him to take at such moments.
>
> In ten minutes, at most, the drug would take effect and he would relax, gradually becoming languid and a little vague, as though after a sleepless night.

Here, at p. 118 of *Le Président*, Balzac would take leave of Simenon. In his own telling of the story it would already be p. 400, since such an addition to his *scènes de la vie politique* would require Balzac to retrace the ex-Premier's whole career, sketching in his background, his love affairs, etc., and describing the architecture and fittings of his converted Norman farmstead in the fullest detail. Balzac's grand old man would make the phone call to Paris—so enabling the novelist to stage one of his great acts of annihilation. Alternatively, he would have confronted the two men.

In either case, Balzac would have treated his readers to public drama, whereas Simenon treats them to a private change of heart. In this sense he is right to maintain that his book has nothing to do with Clemenceau. The fact that Simenon can, in a few lines, suggest all the splendours and miseries of the Third Republic, its moral tawdriness, the lobbying and double-dealing, the display of fake emotion in the Chamber and the Senate, everything implied by Lloyd George's comment on the shabby treatment meted out to Clemenceau at the hands of his compatriots—all this is only a part of his expertise. It belongs, so I imagine he would argue in all modesty, to his stagecraft as a writer. It also belongs to his general knowledge as an intelligent human-being who knows how the world manipulates itself and particularly to his background as a journalist. This is a chapter in Simenon's life that should never be discounted. It took more than writing those scores of centime-thrillers to give him his edge as a critic of society. The author of *Le Président* in 1958 was the same man as the young journalist who reported the Stavisky scandal—the biggest affair of its kind since Panama—for *Paris-Soir* more than twenty years before. (*Reported*, not impressionistically described; the impression of Stavisky in the dock and of the courtroom scene around him is to be found, unforgettable as a Daumier cartoon in the writings of Colette.) The rendering of actual life comes easily to Simenon: it is something he does with his left hand or, to return to our original metaphor, with the other side of his head. The deftness with which he manipulates the men and women who surround his tragedies is seemingly effortless, though its effect upon the reader is that of watching a champion figure-skater or Picasso drawing on glass.

Le Président is an extreme example of Simenon and Sim in close collaboration. Dionysian Simenon, the Simenon of inspiration, the Spinner of Fates and handler of the Furies, is concerned with the individual and the presentation of an individual destiny.

Because men and women cannot be individuals by themselves and can only achieve their destinies in the context of society, Apollonian Sim, Sim, *faber et artifex*, narrator, creator, preserver, must relate a story and supply a background. In *Le Président* it is Sim, the master of suspense and prince of tribal tale-tellers, who holds the tribal reader's interest. Standing in the rain in the courtyard of the Elysée, a skilful journalist asks Chalamont the seemingly innocent yet terrible question, 'Aren't you intending to spend the night upon the road?'

> The man who put that question had known that it would fling Chalamont into confusion.
>
> At this moment the arbiter of his fate was an old man, cut off from the outside world even more completely than usual owing to an electric failure and a telephone breakdown, who sat in a Louis-Philippe armchair, with the sea beating against the cliff hard by and squalls of wind threatening, at ever-diminishing intervals, to carry away the roof of his house.
>
> Twice, three times, the Premier muttered to himself: 'He won't send anybody . . .'
>
> Then, hesitantly: 'He'll come . . .'
>
> At once he would have liked to take back his words, for he was not so sure. At forty years old, or at fifty, he had still believed himself to be a good judge of men, and would pronounce his verdicts without hesitation or remorse. At the age of sixty he had already been less sure of himself, and now he did no more than grope in the dark for momentary truths.

Will Chalamont come or won't he? That is the foreground situation—the situation that Balzac would have exploited and resolved in his own sovereign and dramatic manner. For Simenon it is no more than a narrative device—a device he handles perfectly while concentrating the intensity of his vision on the ex-Premier himself.

> . . . He had begun to hoard his life. He felt he had a whole lot of problems left to solve, not only with calm and composure, but in the completely dispassionate mood that he could achieve only at night, in bed.
>
> This was the most secret of all his tasks, concerning no one except himself; he would have liked to finish it before taking his departure, leaving nothing obscure, looking everything straight in the face. Was it not to help himself in this that he had begun to read so many volumes of memoirs, confessions, private diaries?

Coming to the end of one of these books he was invariably disappointed, irritated, feeling the author had cheated. He wanted pure truth, truth in the raw, as he was trying to find it in his own case, even if it turned out to be sickening or repugnant.

But all the writers he had come across had *arranged* their material, he was far enough on in life to know that. All of them held, believed they held, or pretended to hold, a truth, and he, despite his grim search for truth, had not found it.

Once he has given up his search for truth, the old man can face death in a different fashion. If he is serene, it is for the sad and simple reason that his mind has emptied itself.

It was a strange impression, agreeable and a little terrifying, not needing to think any longer.

A few more flames, a few pages writhing and then falling to ashes between the tongs, and all threads would be severed . . .

'Are you asleep?' Milleran inquired anxiously, noticing all of a sudden that his eyes were closed.

He shook his head, raised his lids, smiled at her as though she were not only Milleran, but the whole of the human race.

'No, my child.'

He added, after a moment's silence: 'Not yet.'

A perfect close, the more so because it is without a moral. As always, Simenon remains the refuser of answers.

Again, take *Les Anneaux de Bicêtre*, a far more static novel than *Le Président*, not only because most of the events take place in the hospital patient's memory but because, at a first reading, it is hard to see why the mind of René Maugras, aged fifty-four, the editor-in-chief of a French national newspaper, should arouse much interest in the reader. True, Maugras has a number of distinguished cronies. He has, in fact, suffered a stroke in the WC of the Grand Véfour, during one of their famous Tuesday luncheons, attended by Chabaud, the great *bâtonnier* of the Paris Bar, two Academicians and his own doctor, Besson, a distinguished medico and society lecher. Yet Maugras himself, as Simenon emphasizes throughout the book, is not a remarkable human being. Professionally, he is not even a brilliant journalist. Toughness, persistence and above all, flair—early in his career, for nosing out a good news story, subsequently for projecting it on the average reader's imagination—these are the qualities that have got him to the top. Now, in his private ward in the Bicêtre

Hospital, screened from the paralytics, geriatrics and occasional lunatics who compose the majority of his fellow-patients, Maugras is auditing his life.

There is really very little to add up. Escape from a drunken father, two unsuccessful marriages, an unwanted daughter—the rest has been hard grind, living and partly living out a success-story that has grown stale even while it is still unfolding. Lying in bed, his eyes fixed on the nurse's white uniform, Maugras hunts through his head for his memories, 'like a child hunting among its toys, choosing which to play with'. Trying to form an opinion about himself and his life, he remembers the priest's words, when he was learning the Catechism:

'Our actions, our speech, our thoughts follow us . . . Nothing is lost . . .'

Now, in the courts where Chabaud spent the best part of his time, a man might be judged in a single day, or in two or three days at most, with the crowd, all round, playing somewhat the same part as the students that surrounded Besson or Audoire when they solemnly made their rounds of the wards.

'I was his schoolteacher . . . At the age of eleven, he already showed a tendency to . . .'

'I am the family doctor . . . I was there at his birth. . . . At three years old . . .'

Then the concierge, the office boss, or somebody or other else would contribute some scrap of truth or error.

The man would sit alone between his two police guards, his chin in his hands, with vacant gaze or with too fixed a stare.

Maugras had no policemen by his sides. There was, indeed, the matron, who would soon be coming to see him and who might well be cast for that part.

Audoire would be the presiding judge, self-assured, impassive, unattackable.

And Besson? One of the assessors. There was always an assessor with rosy cheeks and silvery hair, smiling benevolently after a good lunch.

Lina [his wife] would not be in the court room. Her friends would have told her that her nerves would not stand it. She'd be waiting for news to be given her by telephone, as the case proceeded.

'No! He doesn't look depressed. He seems to have lost interest in what's going on around him . . .'

And Mlle Blanche? Wasn't she the young woman barrister who handed the defendant peppermint drops?

So it continues. Brilliant, effortless, it abounds in incidental vignette and rich characterization—the three nurses, each sharply and perfectly realized, the great specialist ('wouldn't the ideal thing, for some doctors, be sickness without any sick men'), the newspaper-proprietor, still unaccepted by the Jockey Club, the dead poet Jublin and his strange double life, the visit from the barrister and his highly dubious request. If one goes on to declare this the most depressing book that Simenon has ever written—and I am in shameful disagreement here with many Simenonian enthusiasts—it is not merely because, like many library-book seekers, I dislike reading about illness, or even because, in this book more than in any of his others, we have Simenon without Sim, but because Maugras himself is such a lifeless human-being. His mind is a *tabula rasa*, a mirror for whatever passes before his vision or in his memory, one who, to adapt the phrase applied to Mark Pattison, has defecated his character to a pure transparency. With his bundle of ailments, paltry lusts and feeble memories, he is a sitting target for the indignant moralist who insists that Simenon's fundamental attitude to human beings is behaviouristic.

Yet Maugras, like all of us, has had his intimations of immortality. Twice in his adult life—once on a Sunday in the country with his first wife, once by himself by the Mediterranean —he has stepped inside the rings of happiness (hence the book's title?).

> By chance, as at Orléans, he had climbed, not into a little train but into a ramshackle coach full of the twang of Southern accents. He saw the great white squares of the salt pans, the pyramids of salt glistening in the light.
>
> 'Are you going as far as the "Tour Fondue"?'
>
> He stayed in the coach and, at the foot of a rock, a white boat with a yellow funnel was waiting to carry passengers over to the island of Porquerolles. The captain was wearing a sun-helmet. Hampers full of cackling hens were stacked up on the deck.
>
> When the boat slid away from its moorings he stood in the bows, leaning over the transparent water. For a long time he was able to see down to the bottom and for the space of half an hour he lived in music, as though at the heart of a symphony.
>
> That morning was like nothing he had ever experienced since.

It was his great discovery of the world, of a boundless, radiant world
of bright colours and thrilling sounds . . .
He had often been back to the Mediterranean seaboard. He had
seen other seas equally blue, trees and flowers that were more extraordinary, but the magic had gone, and of all his discoveries, this was
the only one to have left a trace.

If this passage sounds contrived or theatrical, productive of the
kind of effect that Priestley has managed so perfectly in plays like
Music at Night or *Johnson over Jordan*, this is because (a) Simenon
so seldom depicts moments of happiness and (b) because happiness
is an irrational state. Lying in bed, remembering, Maugras
forgets his nurse and the daily round of the hospital.

'It's nearly time, Monsieur Maugras . . .'
He gave a start, for he had forgotten Mlle. Blanche and Bicêtre.
'Time for what?'
She realized that he had been a long way off.
'For your temperature . . . And then your purée . . . And soon time
for me to go . . . I promise I won't forget the diary . . .'
The diary? Of course! What would he write in it tonight, if he
had it there? How would he sum up those two plunges into the past?
Cléry. Porquerolles.
Water, both times, and sunshine, heat, fresh smells. And both
times, too, irrational panic and a sullen homeward journey.
Perhaps one word would be enough for both these adventures?
Innocence.
Was twice in a lifetime enough?

Les Anneaux de Bicêtre was written only five years ago, when
Simenon was nearing sixty. For those who resent what they
regard as the author of first-class *romans policiers* setting himself
up as a writer of 'serious' fiction, much as comedians are supposed
to wish to play Hamlet, this final stab at the novel would seem a
fitting conclusion to his ambitions. Indeed, it does mark an end of
a period of Simenon's life as a writer, though, as we shall see,
it is only one that leads on to later and far more singular achievements. Here I shall only remark that the moral truth of this book,
if indeed it has one, is, as is usual in all Simenon's works, oblique,
and that it takes the form of a major psychological observation
thrown off casually in the patient's mind as he lies in bed. Maugras,
we read, 'was fifty-four years old and as he fell asleep that night

he wondered whether one ever really becomes an adult'. This implied conclusion—that no man is ever an adult to himself— is one of the most powerful psychological assertions that Simenon has ever made. Once we have grasped his meaning, it explains almost all his male characters—not only the supposedly unbalanced 'Kiki' Donadieu, but his flabby brother Michel and even his father, Oscar, the powerful dynast-shipowner. It explains Michel Maudet, but it also explains Ferchaux and Alavoine and M. Labbé, the mad hatter of La Rochelle. It certainly explains the Watchmaker of Everton and M. Monde ('A child grown old. Is a man anything more that that?') Above all, as we shall see when we reach his redoubtable and solacing presence, it explains Maigret. It is all the more ironic—yet another example of Simenonian paradox—that this casual truth in the mind of Maugras should relate effectively to almost every major character in Simenon's repertory except Maugras himself.

Just as he refuses to answer their problems, Maugras's along with the others, so Simenon betrays no desire to extend his characters beyond the grave—certainly not down the cold corridors of Purgatory or even, except in a spirit of ironic contradiction, through the lives of their children. Obviously there is such a thing as heredity and Simenon, a lifetime amateur student of medicine and medical theory, would be the last to gainsay its importance. Yet it is more often environment or accident that start his men and women on their desperate paths. Violent reaction or an even more terrifying acquiescence—either an active or a passive principle may set the unlikely fate in motion. It is reaction to their petty provincial backgrounds that drive Michel Maudet and Philippe Dargens to Paris and out to their undiscovered ends. On the other hand, Joseph Dupuche's acceptance of his appalling situation—left high and dry in Panama's Negro quarter with no money and no job and forcibly separated from his frigid but desirable young wife—*creates* for him a destiny no less impressive than the hands dealt out to the two other young men. Outwardly, at a first reading, *Quartier Nègre* is one of the most sombre of Simenon's novels, which is saying a good deal. For those who read his books as a form of catharsis, a release from their own personal terrors (and I suspect that Simenon has far more readers of this kind than one imagines), this little-known work must be one of the most effective outside the major canon. If *La Neige était sale* is the cruellest of his active nightmares, *Quartier Nègre* is its passive complement. Dupuche, with his young Negro mistress, whom he marries when his wife has finally left him, and his breed of half-caste children, three black, two mulatto and the last 'almost white', living in a shanty hut on a dirty beach behind the railway, his body and brain rotted by forbidden native liquor, is a miserable figure, a *raté* of the first order. His existence is a veritable nightmare, an invitation to bad dreams. It even scares the waking thoughts of those by no means scareable individuals who make up Simenon's French colony.

Yet, like all Simenon's nightmares, Dupuche's destiny has a saving grace. (Perhaps to call it 'saving grace' confuses the issue. The fates that preside over Simenonian destinies bear no relation to the coven of demented Mother Superiors who weave the tangled webs that involve the characters of Claudel's dramas or the novels of Greene and Bernanos.) Though Simenon never grudges his men and women a journey to the end of the night, the end, once arrived at, is seldom quite so terrible as it has seemed in the reader's imagination while the tragedy was unfolding; this may be yet another contradiction. In *Quartier Nègre*, for example, Simenon spares Dupuche and the reader nothing in the way of squalor and humiliation. Yet the finish, when it comes—as it does abruptly in a page and a half, in the official-notification manner characteristic of much classic Russian fiction—is so drily managed as to be almost an anti-climax. Once again, Dupuche's creator has refused an answer to the riddle of his hero's black-comedy existence. All that we can say is that Joseph Dupuche, late of Amiens, a hard-working average young engineer with a widowed, exigent mother and a prudish, less-than-average wife has, through no fault of his own, been plunged into an abyss—and emerged, a contented beachcomber. 'Look, we have come through!'—as Lawrence put it—at a cost!

I think that it is this feeling of anti-climax that has led Brigid Brophy, one of Simenon's most acute critics, to speak of the 'top-heaviness' of his fiction. 'Probably,' she writes,

> . . . . it comes from the resolute defeatism, the low relief, of his vision. Since this is implicit in the very manner of his writing from the start, it makes for an overloading of the first third of the book; a little too much of the conclusion is already stated in the major premise. The conclusion therefore doesn't carry quite the right weight, doesn't make quite the decisive home-coming click of surprise plus inevitability. To work, as Simenon determinedly does, with a mute—a rainy—palette invites the same difficulties about the moment of home-coming as singing in a minor key. Simenon is too versed a craftsman to go sour on the key note, but one senses his having to feel around for it; he comes to it, finally, with not quite enough breath.

In *Le Train*, Miss Brophy goes on, the writer, 'achieves perfect breath control'. Yet, with all respect, is this really so? Given the artistry and the perfect composition of *Le Train*, what does Marcel's moral failure really amount to? The time is summer, 1940, the place a town in north-eastern France. Timid, short-sighted, middle-aged, ex-tubercular, Marcel has closed his radio repair shop, dumped his poultry on the neighbours and fled, with his pregnant wife and young daughter, along with the other refugees. He is separated from his family, he finds himself in a refugee reception camp, he has a love affair. Miss Brophy describes it as 'one of the most poignant love affairs in twentieth-century literature', though, personally, I can think of twenty love affairs —in Maigret's experience, let alone in Simenon's works as a whole—that are every whit as poignant as this episode. Marcel, Miss Brophy writes sadly and regretfully, 'cannot rise to the occasion of his love affair and transcend his marriage'. But of course not. He is Marcel—the Marcel we have come to know in the crowded cattle-truck, as the train makes its long, stumbling journey across France under the blue summer skies of 1940. Of course Marcel will continue to search for his wife and of course he will find her. The climax—Marcel's later meeting with the girl, now a Resistance member on the run from the Nazis, his refusal to shelter her and her subsequent death at the hands of a firing squad—all this is no climax at all, merely M. Sim's way of clinching the story. Basically, *Le Train* is a Tchekovian episode—the most important episode in Marcel's life. If Simenon does achieve 'perfect breath control' in this book, he does so artificially, making an artistic virtue out of a tragic vacuum. Since the elements of a genuine Simenon-Sim situation or 'destiny' are lacking, the equation is false and completes itself mechanically. Tchekov's country lane has turned into the Rue Maupassant, that well-known urban *cul-de-sac*.

I have chosen this last instance as an example of how no two readers of Simenon can think about his books along the same lines of feeling. For every fifty of us who read Sim 'for his story-teller's gift of wanting to know "what happens next" ', for every twenty who read Simenon-Sim with the pleasurable self-satisfaction that in savouring the collaborative balance between the two they can legitimately claim to be 'enjoying' literature, there must be at least two who read Simenon as a form of therapy and at least one, if we are to believe François Mauriac, who puts off reading his works, not for any theological reason, but simply out of funk. ('I have begun reading a fine Simenon,' Mauriac ruefully admits in his *Bloc-Notes*, 'but I fear I lack the courage to plumb to the depths of this nightmare which he describes with such intolerable art.') No sensitive reader of Simenon can deny that he has shared Mauriac's lack of courage. As I said earlier, the sensation is generally uppermost on Page One. In the second paragraph of *L'Horloger d'Everton*, for example, we are told that this Saturday evening was the last Dave Galloway was to spend as a happy human being. The reason that we are so unwillingly compelled and hypnotized into following Dave and his co-sufferers into the heart of tragedy is simply, as Miss Brophy rightly says, because

> . . . he makes the habits and idiosyncrasies of his characters so known to the reader that each and every reader emotionally equates the character with the person of his most intimate acquaintance, himself. Similarly, localities realized in such exact and penetrating detail can be treated by the reader's emotions only as the one locality we have all apprehended in truly vivid detail, the setting of our childhood.

This is the simple but essential secret of Simenon's art and of its complexity, the secret of his protean shape as a novelist. Like all great writers of fiction, he has the actor's temperament (*'Madame Bovary, c'est moi!'*). All his life he has been not just observing but *simulating* men and women: their loves, deliriums, obsessions, the secret hiding places of their minds, their urge towards self-realization or self-destruction. Above all, he has imagined and lived through his characters' loneliness. Yet in the first analysis, it is observation, the faithful observation of particulars, that is the groundwork of his fiction. And so, with *Pedigree*, that autobiographical Baedeker, in hand as a guide to Simenon's first sixteen years, we can attempt a brief sketch of his life as a writer.

Chapter 2

PEDIGREE

AT a first glance—unless one is interested in the nineteenth-century industrial scene or the civic history of the Middle Ages—Liège is not a place to linger in. To the stranger who arrives by train from the north-east, the city, ringed by its slag-heaps and coal-tips, presents an aspect of laborious lifelessness that only increases when one leaves the railway station. A strange and unpleasant smell, compound of coal dust, gas and frying fat, hangs strongly everywhere, even on the jungly but apparently uninhabited urban heights where nothing seems to have stirred since the 1918 Armistice and where, in the early evening, the visitor can wander for fifteen minutes at a time without glimpsing another human being, except for a suspicious, disapproving face peering from behind a curtained window, without hearing any immediate sound save the ring of his own footsteps on the pavement. A stale, stagnant, take-it-or-leave-it atmosphere pervades this citadel of the Walloon and Flemish bourgeoisie. If Liège, as I suspect, has a huge and guilty secret shared in common by its inhabitants, it is not giving it away, even to commercial travellers.

Like all the most hideous cities of Europe—and it has, not without reason, though specifically on account of its long connection with the armaments industry, been named 'the Birmingham of the Low Countries'—Liège is highly and publicly self-conscious. It is almost as if the city were apologizing to the stranger in advance for all the Home-and-Colonial human exploitation that it represents—the collieries and factories close at hand which the young of half a century ago 'usually glimpsed only from the train, dark and mysterious, with the bloody maws of their furnaces being fed by half-naked demons', and the distant, horrific Congo of Leopold II. On the grimly conformist ridges of redbrick above the city centre, remembrance is heavily ecclesiastical. At almost every street corner a rectangular plaque in white and black enamel recalls the existence of some unbending Prince-Bishop of the ninth, tenth or eleventh centuries—an Evariste or Childeric, '*Evêque et Martyr*', or plain *Evêque* without the palm. In the main streets down below, botanists and mathematicians, historians and civil engineers are commemorated. As one turns into the Rue César Franck—the ugliest street in the world to be named after a great composer—a tablet proclaims that '*Ici Isy Colin, poète Liègeois, composa ses premiers vers*'; somehow one knows those lachrymose verses, a mixture of Lamartine and milky water, without having read them. The answer to it all would seem to be a large aspidistra and indeed, in their heavy brass pots, these are in much residential evidence. The municipal architecture is Holborn Prudential Gothic without the grandeur of conception, the cafés and restaurants substantial but depressing. Even the pubs exude a wary, hang-dog hospitality that consorts more with secret than with public drinking.

Everything in Liège seems to have been run up pretentiously yet on the cheap, every service performed grudgingly yet with unction; this is particularly noticeable if one has travelled to it from Amsterdam, that queen of cities and haven of Northern Europe's civilized amenities. The very flowers in the drab and dusty but numerous public places seem to have been doled out by a sparing hand and then stuck in the ground like so many bits of coloured metal. The citizens of Liège present a joyless, abrupt and indifferent collective face to the world, a sad but determined last-century face, pinched and sharpened by last-century virtues and vices—avarice, hard work, hypocrisy, thrift and pretension— the face in fact, in its better moments, of Roger Mamelin's mother, the Elise of *Pedigree*. Given much rebuilding, buses in place of trams and electricity instead of gas, the city's personality seems scarcely to have changed since Simenon's birth there more than sixty years ago.

Pedigree, published in 1948, is less an autobiographical novel than a vast chunk of autobiography four times as long as the average Simenon novel, in which some of the characters have been rearranged and several incidents invented. Simenon originally began it as a plain record of his childhood told in the first person and addressed to his young son, after a doctor 'on the basis of an inaccurate X-ray, informed me that I had at the most two years to live'. Intending to give his son an account of his father's family and early life, he published the first hundred pages under the title of *Je me souviens* in 1945. At his friend Gide's bidding, he later recast these chapters in the third person and completed the book in the form of fiction. In a second recasting, after a succession of writs issued by persons who thought themselves to have been libelled in the narrative, he omitted everything that might be considered offensive. He allows that the character of Roger Mamelin has 'a great deal in common with the child I once was' and that 'everything is true while nothing is accurate'. Yet Roger and his parents are indistinguishable from the three Simenons in the earlier version while the dates, places, schooling and general background to Roger's life correspond with everything that is known of Simenon's own early life and chronology. Substantially, we may take *Pedigree* to be a highly detailed and wonderfully observant self-portrait.

Georges Joseph Christian Simenon was born at No. 10, Rue Léopold, shortly after 1 a.m. on the morning of Friday, February 13, 1903. Alarmed by the date of the month and the day of the week, Henriette Simenon persuaded her husband to make a false declaration at the Town Hall, stating that the birth occurred before midnight on the 12th. On the very threshold of life, as it were, Simenon pulled off his first stroke of ambiguity. His father, Désiré Simenon, was twenty-five and his mother, *née* Brull, was twenty-two.

Originally, the Simenons came from Brittany. One of them, a soldier in the Grande Armée of 1812, dropped out of the line of march during the long and terrible crawl back from Russia at a place called Vlijtijen in Belgian Limbourg, settled there, married and raised a family. Chrétien Simenon, Georges's grandfather, was a hatter, a skilled craftsman, who had begun his working life travelling through Europe—Germany, France, Italy, Switzerland —as a journeyman-apprentice. Désiré Simenon, the writer's father (the Désiré of the novel) was the head clerk of a small insurance company. When his employer asked him to choose between life and fire, the two branches of the firm's business, he chose, very typically, to handle the fire policies since it was the more concrete and less complicated alternative—'a quiet business involving only very rare calls on clients. It was at that moment that life insurance had started forging ahead'. Consequently Désiré, though nominally in charge of the office with power of attorney and access to the safe combination, earns far less commission than his colleague in the 'Life' department. It is the first of Elise's manifold reproaches:

> 'I can't understand why a man who is far less intelligent than you are should earn more than you do, in your own office.'
> 'Good luck to him. Have we ever gone short of anything?'
> 'It seems he even drinks.'
> 'What he does outside the office is no concern of ours.'
> And the word 'office', in Mamelin's mind, had a capital letter. He loved his big ledgers, and his eyes sparkled when, with his lips quivering slightly and his finger running down the columns, he did a sum, faster than anybody else, as all his colleagues agreed. They recognized too that he had never made a mistake. That was not just idle talk. It was an act of faith.

Tranquil, serene even, upright, diligent, and entirely unambitious, Désiré lives for the apparent moment. To Elise (Henriette Simenon) he appears unfeeling, insouciant. ' "You know, poor little Valérie," she tells her friend, "a man doesn't feel things as we do . . ." because he did what he could, all that he could, and considered the rest would be given him into the bargain.' In fact, as the reader only learns some three hundred pages later, when his wife asks him, 'Don't you think you ought to take out a life-insurance policy?', Désiré has a heart condition which he has discussed with no one but the firm's doctor. He has long known that it is impossible for him to insure his own life.

> She believed, she had always believed, that he had no antennae . . .
> He went on walking along in silence and she was a long way from suspecting that this question, which she had finally put after a long shudder of her whole body, was a question which he had been expecting for a long time, for months, perhaps for years, and that his blood had frozen in his veins.
> All the same, he managed to say in a normal voice, with scarcely any sign of strain in it: 'Why are you asking me about that today?'
> 'I wanted to talk to you about it before.'

How could she explain that it was the sight of Charles in mourning, the memory of Françoise's eyes, and her conversation with Madame Dossin who was suffering from tuberculosis, which had given her, by means of heaven knows what circuitous associations, an unbearable longing for security? It all went much further back, in fact, to the years spent in a dirty back street with her mother, to the empty saucepans they used to put on the stove, to Monsieur Marette's suicide, to the hours spent with Madame Pain on the bench in the Place du Congrès. Even the newspapers, which no longer talked of anything but war and catastrophes, had helped to crystallize her fears . . .

Meanwhile, fresh, immaculate, 'as if he were acting in a play', Désiré goes out to a new day at the office, 'sweeping his hat off to people he knew'.

His neighbours could tell what time it was without looking at their alarm-clocks. Shopkeepers taking down their shutters knew whether they were early or late; but Désiré went by, swinging his legs along at such a regular pace that you might have thought they had been given the task of measuring the passage of time. He scarcely ever stopped on the way. People and things did not seem to interest him and yet he smiled beatifically. He was sensitive to the quality of the air, to slight changes in temperature, to distant sounds, to moving patches of sunlight. The taste of his morning cigarette varied from day to day and yet they were all cigarettes of the same brand, cork-tipped 'Louxors' . . .
. . . He had handsome, sparkling brown eyes, a big Cyrano-de-Bergerac nose, and a turned-up moustache; his hair, which was brushed back, and his bald temples gave him a high forehead.
'A poet's forehead,' Elise used to say.

Elise could be described as the heroine of the first two-thirds of *Pedigree*. Simenon's portrait of her—as wife, mother, relative, neighbour and keeper of a lodging-house—is unforgettable. She is touching, exasperating, pitiful, frail yet indestructible, all, as it were, together and in the same breath. Tearful, apologetic, anxious, always smiling nervously, always expecting the worst, a born complainer who is never so infuriating as when she is manifestly refraining from complaint, she is among the great women-martyrs of literature, the complete contrast to her outwardly stolid, optimistic, good-natured and long-suffering husband.

But Désiré and Elise are not only contrasted human beings in themselves. Each of them represents the conflicting habits and principles of their respective families. The Mamelins are Walloons, embedded in the working-class Outremeuse district of Liège, clannish, plebeian, 'hungry at every hour of the day', living merrily in 'that vulgar, cordial disorder in which they were all so happy', 'in which they were *wallowing*' as Elise describes them. And just as no one in the Mamelin family kitchen in the Rue Puits-en-Sock has much time for Elise, the anaemic, the refined, the thirteenth child 'who had no money and no health' and can scarcely feed her own baby, so none of the Peters family have ever taken to Big Désiré. For the Peters (Brull) family is Flemish. Elise's father, the well-to-do son of a German landowner, married to a rich Dutch farmer's daughter, was once a big man in the Limbourg district—a *dijkmeester* (an honorary surveyor of dykes and controller of waterways), a timber merchant with ten horses in his stables and a string of barges. Sitting in her kitchen with her eldest brother, the ne'er-do-well alcoholic Léopold (here Simenon has given full rein to his imagination), Elise questions him about their family. She learns how the elder Peters took to drink, signed bills of exchange, went bankrupt. She herself was forced to take a job as a shop-assistant at the Liège store of L'Innovation (it still exists), and it was here that she first met Désiré. Interrogating Léopold, so inscrutable and oracular in drink, yet so strangely impressive and so much older than herself, she relives the Peters' glories.

> . . . she was just as timid in front of him, who could talk about the past, as she would have been in front of a witch that could predict the future . . .
>
> She wanted to know more. She was afraid of all that Léopold knew and yet she was also afraid of seeing him go, she needed to question him, to feed on the Peters' past, on their history, on their life.
>
> How far away was the hat-shop in the Rue Puits-en-Sock, and even big Désiré sitting behind the green windows of the insurance office!

Elise's tireless, genteel timidity, her humble smile, her simpering apologies, her eternal whining about the state of her 'organs', about how Désiré only earns 'the bare necessities of life', conceal an ant-like industry and an iron will—a Peters will, far stronger than that of the apparently robust Mamelins.

Did she already sense that she was stronger than they were, strong in her weeping eyes, in her pale, hollow cheeks, in her aching belly, in the iron prescribed for her anaemia, in her legs which kept giving way on the stairs, did she know, the little Fleming, the thirteenth-born of the Peters, what she wanted and where she was going?

She had been married for barely two years. She had always said yes to everything, but this particular Sunday because it was necessary, because a strange force was impelling her, because she was a Peters and there were Mamelins in the world, because life was in command, she was going to fight, and fight with her own weapons.

She moves her family—as the Simenons did, in fact, move—out of Désiré's agreeable rut in the Rue Léopold to a house in the Rue de la Loi, facing Roger's first school, the Institut St. André. Here, in face of Désiré's disapproval, she begins to take in lodgers, mostly indigent Poles and Russians studying at the university. She cheats them ('clips' them, as she calls it), merci-lessly, a centime here, a centime there, filling their coal-buckets with short measure, helping herself out of their tins of coffee. She cheats her husband in the same way. Each week she takes the sum she has saved from her clippings out of the pink soup-tureen and banks it in Roger's account. All because 'she did not want to be poor. The very sight of poverty made her sick with fear and disgust. She hated the rich but she did not like the poor'. Elise is hell-bent on security and the world's esteem for the pair of them, mother and son. She is determined to make a Peters of Roger, though in her moments of greatest anxiety she hardly knows what that talisman implies: 'I sometimes wonder, Léopold, if in our family, we aren't quite like other people.'

In the Rue Puits-en-Sock, all those little shopkeepers who had been born side by side and would die side by side, next door to one another, lived together like a big family, without any worries, and that was why she had an involuntary feeling of irritation every time she saw Désiré setting off with Roger for his father's hat-shop.

Scattered all over the place, and strangers in their own district, the Peters instinctively drew towards one another, because only one of their own family could understand them; but, once they were together, they kept quiet as if they were frightened of their daemon. . . . Was there a race of human beings more sensitive than the rest, who suffered more and whom nothing could satisfy?

At first, prompted by her elder sister, Louisa ('it was there, in that layer of hypocritical kindness and bigotry, that the idea had originated'), Elise sees Roger, always top of his class at the Christian Brothers, as a priest (as the verse goes, 'when you become a priest, I shall be your servant'). She badgers the Jesuits, ever on the look-out for clever boys from poor homes, into taking him into the Collège St. Louis for half fees. Later, as a result of precocious sexual curiosity—his first adventure with a girl occurs when he is not yet thirteen—Roger throws up the priesthood and decides to become an army officer. 'You understand, Louisa,' Elise tells her sister, 'if he hasn't got the vocation, we can't force him. There's nothing worse than a bad priest. As an officer, he'll have a safe career, and once they've won their epaulettes they've got nothing to worry about.' Finally, lowering her sights, she dreams of a cake-shop where 'a sturdy, good-natured Roger would toil away in the scented warmth of the bakehouse while she herself, neat and trim in an embroidered white apron crackling with starch, would serve tarts across a marble counter'.

The novel ends just after the 1918 Armistice. By that time Roger is in his sixteenth year. His father's ill-health has forced him to give up his studies and find a job (Simenon did, in fact, do a fortnight's stint at a pastrycook's and served for six weeks as a bookseller's assistant, leaving for the same reason as does Roger in the novel—namely, because he knew more about Dumas' works than his employer and was forced into politely contradicting him in front of a customer).

As an arranged autobiography *Pedigree* is an extraordinary book. Simenon succeeds magnificently in imposing a whole lost world upon the reader. Roger's parents themselves are wonderfully presented, as are the individual members of the Mamelin and Peters families, their husbands, wives, cousins and in-laws and the network of surrounding human-beings—students, shopkeepers, priests, charwomen, office-clerks, adolescent street girls and the rest. Simenon's technique in this book is not so much impressionistic as *pointilliste*—the total effect of a vast social tableau is achieved by a piling-on of details, an accumulation of atmospheric touches. The Agadir crisis, the Belgian General Strike, a fire, a parish feast-day, an anarchist outrage (Liège was a dynamiters' playground before and during this period), the outbreak of the Great War, the German Occupation—each public event is seen in microcosm as it affects the Mamelin household and the inhabitants of the Rue Puits-en-Sock. M. Charles of the Belgian Deuxième Bureau, the plump, pot-bellied police spy, politely ironic in his inquiries after Elise's lodger, Frida Stavitskaia, and Mlle Frida herself, greasy and unwashed, a student tearaway involved in the assassination of a Russian Grand Duke, are merely the local understudies of a period 'great game' being played out on a larger scale elsewhere. It is this that makes the book such a quiet but effective social document. The truth of Simenon's totally depressive picture of his native city lies in the limitation of his general judgments. The method is objective, observing what the eye sees, the ear hears, the senses respond to: the condemnation is implicit. Simenon's presentation of *petit-bourgeois* society in the first decade of the century— a society in which all or most human values and dignities have been corroded or swallowed up in rabid materialism, anxiety and pretension—is twice as deadly for being so sharply parochial and intimate. Once again we have the universal—this time a universal drawn out of history—localized in the particular.

In the world of *Pedigree* religion, patriotism and what, for want of a better expression, one might call secular piety, are all at an itemized discount. However careful Simenon is to keep priests out of his fiction proper, sketches of clerical and semi-clerical life abound in *Pedigree*. Thus, we have Charles Daigne, the hushing-and-shooshing sacristan, epitome of all Levite hangers-on; the purple-faced Dean of St. Nicholas 'as common as a tobacco-jar', always harking back to his dinner; Father van Bambeek, the hulking ex-cavalry officer who has turned Jesuit Prefect of Discipline and exchanged polo for charity bazaars; Brother Mésnard, with his wooden leg and his ambiguous advances. Only the suffering, palely smiling Father Renchon is anything like a priest after the order of Melchizedech. Gallant little Belgium herself is represented by M. Dollent, the young hospital intern and reservist, killed on the first evening of the Great War 'in that forest of Sart-Tilmant, near Boncelles, where they had so often gone picnicking, and where two regiments of riflemen would wipe each other out, each mistaking the other for the enemy'. The pieties, generally represented by the small craftsmen of the Outremeuse district, centre around Roger's grandfather, the hatter. All three sets of values coalesce in Roger's father, who might well have been named Résigné rather than Désiré Mamelin, for his whole life is one of happy and tranquil resignation. Alone among the huge cast that Simenon has assembled, he is the willing victim of the society he embodies, accepting its shams and hypocrisies at their face-value with child-like innocence—an innocence that he has been unable to transmit to his preternaturally observant and receptive son.

And it is here, perhaps, that *Pedigree* may legitimately be said to fail as a work of art. 'Legitimately' because the professed aim of the book, under any of its guises, is to record Roger's first sixteen years and in this it succeeds perfectly. All too faithfully, in fact, since in tracing Roger's line of development from the watchful child aware of everything around him to the furious scene-creating adolescent, frustrated by his family, his abortive schooling, his need of sex, his comparative poverty and loathing of his better-off schoolmates, the artistic unity of the first two-thirds of the book is lost. The foreground of Roger's self-discovery swamps the rich landscape of environment; in the same structural, but in a very different psychological, sense as the first and perfect two hundred pages of David Copperfield's childhood are swamped by the long plot and counter-plot contrivances of David's subsequent narrative. For those who think that Simenon's account of his youth is far too long already—and, as we shall see, such readers include Maigret himself!—it may sound absurd to suggest that the book would have been improved by adding another couple of hundred pages. Yet only in this way could the artificial foreshortening of the last third of *Pedigree* have been avoided.

The plain fact is that Roger, given his time, circumstances and locale, is no more interesting or original than any other thwarted and intelligent adolescent, except as he enables us to realize the background of Simenon's own childhood and youth—not, as M. Parinaud would have it, to find there the source of all his subsequent genius, but rather to record the setting and starting-point of his observation of human beings. If *Pedigree* is unlike any of his other books, it is primarily because in this case it is the surround and not the protagonist that counts. To rediscover the book again after a long interval is to realize that it is Elise herself and Liège itself that one remembers most vividly. Those who read Greek tragedy often tell us that their highest reach of enjoyment comes with the Chorus. So, for myself, the high point of *Pedigree* is to be found in such moments as that in which Simenon describes the group of old men making their way to the public baths for their morning dip, disjointedly mumbling about the threat of war, 'and what the Swedes intend and what the French'—or, in this case, M. Fallières and Kaiser Wilhelm.

> . . . every day they met at the same time, coming from different points of the compass, as if they attracted each other like magnets, and their little band grew bigger as a band of schoolboys grows bigger as it approaches the school . . .
> They were all between sixty and seventy years old. They had reached the top of their careers. They no longer expected any surprises from life, and, every day, they walked along with measured tread, in the cool morning air, past the shuttered houses in which people were still asleep . . .
> It was the time of day when a scented mist rose from the glistening river, the barges coated with shining pitch slowly moved away from the banks, and the tugs hooted and shuddered with impatience outside the Coronmeuse lock. It was also the time when the nearby slaughterhouse was full of the sound of bellowing and the animals being driven along the embankment bumped into one another in the roadway.
> Roger did not listen to the old men's conversation. They talked very little, relaxing in long, heavy silences. You could feel that they had a language of their own, like little children, a language which only they could understand, after the forty years or so they had known each other.
> They had become friends long ago, when they were thin, ambitious young men, when Monsieur Repasse, who was now the shoemaker to high society, was still employed in a little workshop, and Monsieur Pelcat, who had not yet acquired his bulky paunch, used to tour the country fairs as a pedlar.
> True, they had lost sight of one another for a time, while they were working hard and starting families. But then they had come together again on the other slope of existence, and they may well have believed that they were still the same.

If, as Simenon contends, much of his fiction is an attempt to achieve the mood and essence of Greek tragedy in terms of the

twentieth-century novel, these old men of Liège are the fitting
and acceptable variant of a Sophoclean Chorus.

Having discussed and disposed of *Pedigree* and its relevance to
Simenon's early life, we can return to the facts and dates of his
biography proper, based on the admirable summary prefaced to
M. Bernard de Fallois's documentary study of his work. As we
have noted, he survived the pastrycook and the irate bookseller.
In January 1919, he joined the staff of the *Gazette de Liège* as a
cub or junior reporter, graduating from stray or run-over dogs,
through court and municipal reporting, to the editing of a daily
comic column entitled 'From the Hen Roost' signed 'M. le Coq'.
(An earlier assignment with a scandalous news-sheet entitled
La Cravache ['The Horsewhip'] ended abruptly when the youth
discovered that the paper's finances were dependent on blackmail
rather than advertisement and circulation.) An admirer of Mark
Twain and Jerome K. Jerome, young Simenon believed he had
talent as a professional humorist. It was a belief that persisted
long after his writing novitiate was over and has contributed
distressingly to the *kitsch* and horseplay elements that can be
discerned in some of the earliest fiction published under his own
name. He belonged to a set of young poets and painters who
called themselves '*La Caque*' (the tough, cynical, beer-swilling
'Keg' in place of the soft, admiring *claque*?). Some of these
friends were later to illustrate his first novel, a satire on Liège
society entitled *Au Pont des Arches* (1921). To their staid, middle-
aged seniors this band of noisy, self-opinionated provincial
geniuses must have been anathema, their boastful high spirits
insufferable. In fact they were probably no worse than any other
group of their kind. Readers of *Le Pendu de Saint-Pholien*,
which is mainly set in Liège, will recognize what may be a fragment
of Simenon's youth in the 'Companions of the Apocalypse'—
a club of students and painters founded to link Art and Science.
'Each of us,' an ex-member remarks, 'thought he'd be at least
a Rembrandt . . . We used to read a lot, especially writers of the
Romantic period. We'd swear by one writer for a week. Then
we'd drop him and take up another . . . We used to sing old songs
and recite Villon . . . We used to drink. We drank a lot . . . We
used to smoke pipe after pipe . . . We were convinced that people

in the street used to look at us with a mixture of admiration and terror.' All this, without the viciousness that leads to a killing in the novel, would seem to describe the studio atmosphere of '*La Caque*' with fair accuracy. That there was a sadder and seamier side to the lives of several of Simenon's Liège friends at this period can be seen in *Les Trois Crimes de mes Amis* which appears to be largely based on factual experience.

In the winter of 1920–21 Simenon got engaged, and he finally married Regina Renchon at Liège in March 1923. Meanwhile he did eighteen months' military service in the Belgian Army Service Corps; the barracks were near his home and he could still work as a journalist. The day before he began his soldiering, his father collapsed and died at his office desk. Désiré Simenon was aged forty-two when he died. It was only then that Simenon and his mother learned the grim truth about the life-insurance policy that his own company had refused him. For Mme. Simenon, after all her nagging and upbraiding, the shock and remorse at discovering the painful truth that her husband had been sparing her all those years, must have been appalling: in Simenon himself it aroused a hatred of all summary moral judgments passed on human-beings that has remained a permanent feature of his attitude to human character ever since.

He arrived in Paris in the winter of 1922 and took a job as secretary to a M. Binet-Valmer, President of the *Ligue des Chefs de Section et Anciens Combattants*, a powerful old soldiers' organisation with multi-political links that brought him in contact with public figures as differently aligned as Poincaré, Tardieu and Léon Daudet. More importantly, through his employer he met Henri Duvernois, editor of *Le Matin*. Colette, who had achieved fame two years earlier with *Chéri*, was the paper's literary editor and dramatic critic. As a result, its arts pages were the best in French daily journalism. Every Monday *Le Matin* published a short story. Simenon was already pot-boiling furiously for a living (he wrote more than a thousand short stories between 1923 and 1933) but his ambition was to have a contribution accepted by Colette. His first story she refused outright. He persevered until, as he relates in his *Portraits Souvenir*, 'one day I was told, "Madame Colette would like to see you". She was marvellous to behold in her editorial chair, suddenly addressing me as *"Mon petit Sim . . ."* "You know," she said, "I read your last story, and I ought to have returned it weeks ago. It's almost right. It almost works. But not quite. You are too literary. You must not be literary. Suppress all the literature and it will work . . ." That was the most useful advice I've ever had in my life, and I owe a grateful candle to Colette for having given it to me'.

By 1924 Simenon, aged twenty-one, and installed on the ground floor of the Maréchal de Richelieu's town house in the Place des Vosges, was churning out his Knockespotch *romans populaires* (the first of them, *Le Roman d'une Dactylo*, was written on a café terrace in a single morning). Four years later he bought his first boat—a seventeen-foot craft named *Ginette*—and toured France's rivers and canals in her. A year later, on board the *Ostrogoth*—thirty-five-foot long, four times the size of *Ginette*, with a twenty h.p. engine, built at Fécamp and baptised by the Curé of Notre Dame—he anchored off a timber-yard at Delfzijl in the Ems estuary and began to write his first Maigret, *Pietr-le-Letton*, published in 1930. Shortly afterwards he arranged with Fayard to launch Maigret's adventures as a series once a sufficient number had been written. The first eight titles duly appeared in 1931. *Le Passager du 'Polarlys'*, the first non-Maigret novel written under his own name, was published in the following year.

From this point on Simenon's essential life can be said to lie in his books. He becomes the sum of his achievements and a bare chronology suffices. He has travelled in many parts of the world—to French and Belgian Africa in 1932, to the United States, Central and South America, Tahiti, Australasia and the East Indies in 1935. The place-dates of his books read like luggage labels: Porquerolles, Noland, Igls in the Austrian Tyrol, Tumacacori on the Mexican frontier of Arizona, Braderton Beach (Cuba), Carmel-by-the-Sea in California, Lakeville (Connecticut), Cannes, Echandens (Canton de Vaud). He has lived for long periods in La Rochelle, where he organized aid for the refugees in 1940, and in Brittany. He has a powerful liking for London, Rome and Milan, and a strong affection for Edinburgh. After the war he lived for something like ten years in Canada and the United States, returning to Europe as suddenly and apparently as casually as he had left it. He remarried in 1950 and has one son by his first wife, two sons and a daughter by his second marriage.

★

Since 1963 Simenon has lived with his family at Epalinges, a village some ten miles east of Lausanne, in a large roomy white house built to his own design for living, having purchased several acres of surrounding meadowland to prevent anything else being put up in the neighbourhood. With its self-contained electric plant and large indoor swimming-pool (a far cry from the old men's bathing place by the Meuse), it might, at a first glance, be the country home of some intelligent, high-powered and well-to-do New Englander—a Senator say, an ex-Ambassador or Kennedy brainstruster with a Harvard-Rhodes Scholar-Sorbonne education. At least, though I have never been in the States, when an American woman friend of Simenon's asked me, after a visit there, what his home reminded me of, this was the only imaginative picture that occurred to me. 'Warm but no,' she replied, 'try again . . . Doesn't it strike you that that house at Epalinges would be ideal for some kind of clinic?' And she went on to explain how Simenon had told her that he had designed his house in the knowledge that, once his children were grown-up, he would need something a great deal smaller. Hence he had designed a house which, while perfectly suited to his own and his family's needs and comfort, could, in a country famous for its sanatoria, be converted to such clinical use almost overnight. Such a mixture of genial and hospitable concern with the present and businesslike thought for the future is somehow typical of a born pragmatist like Simenon. In life, as in art, he is a masterly and deceptive contriver.

Health, wealth, taste and simplicity is the note of the Simenon household. Everything in it, you feel, from the many beautiful objects to the plainest kitchen utensils, has been included—to adapt Gibbon's immortal description of the Emperor Gordian's establishment—'for use rather than ostentation'.[1]

[1] v. Chapter XLV of *The Decline and Fall of the Roman Empire*: 'Twenty-two acknowledged concubines and a library of sixty-two thousand volumes, attested the variety of his inclinations; and from the productions which he left behind him, it appears that both the one and the other were designed for use rather than for ostentation.'

The pictures and sculpture, all in high relief, are plainly there to be looked at and enjoyed rather than paraded. The view from the forty-odd windows of the house has been left unencumbered so as to rest the eye. The plain white walls and dark red carpets of fitted pile, the abundance of cupboards and play-space, the discreet profusion of labour-saving gadgets and the airy spacious-ness of the domestic quarters all combine to give the visitor the visible and tangible impression of a private Thelema such as a contemporary Rabelais would plan it. It is, you feel, the home of a man who has made immense riches out of his imaginative brain-work and believes in making his century work for him—the proper setting for a writer who aims to keep his own life as smooth, stream-lined and pared down as his fiction.

Thus, for example, there are books in plenty at Epalinges but no more than one would expect: much modern fiction—Faulkner, Moravia, Graham Greene and Steinbeck greatly in evidence—a good deal of random history, a large glass bookcase in the smaller of Simenon's two working studies filled with volumes on medicine and psychiatry, and the complete *Larousse* and *Britannica*. The enviable exceptions to this working library are a superb set of Stendhal in the writer's bedroom (its rich red-leather binding recalls the sumptuous Tacitus that the Bishop gave to Julien Sorel) and, even more covetable, the entire Edition de la Pléiade—that magnificently produced and edited series of French and foreign classics that now totals some two hundred volumes. Simenon, a devoted admirer and subscriber to this publishing dream, receives a copy of each new Pléiade as it appears. On the day I visited him, he had been pleased to welcome two new additions to his library—a Swedish edition of *Striptease*, his Riviera cabaret novel, and the single-volume Pléiade of Gogol. It was hard to tell which had delighted him most—the lurid, sexy cover of his own paperback, so unsuited to the highly sexed but un-wanton Swedes, or the perfection of the Gogol, his favourite author.

This visit to Epalinges was my first meeting with Simenon. One's first impression was that for a man of sixty-four he looked amazingly young for his age, a man who might well be in his late or even middle forties. The word 'spry' has an arch, hackneyed sound and one would not normally choose to employ it. I can only plead that it is the most accurate adjective that I can find to describe Simenon at a first encounter, although perhaps 'relaxed briskness' would be a better expression. His affability and receptiveness, his immense vitality and energy, displayed in speech and movement, are what most immediately strike the visitor.

In my case he gave up a whole afternoon to answering and enlarging upon a host of what must have seemed highly banal questions about his work, his method of writing, conception of character and so on. Having suffered so many interviewers gladly, resignedly, over the last twenty years or so, he has developed an agile technique in dealing with his academic, critical, or journalistic interrogators. It consists largely of a ping-pong-pat method of reply that suggests that his visitor has not only presented him with a highly sympathetic, interesting and original gloss on the obvious, but, in doing so, has somehow at the same time succeeded in raising the one issue that he had long been waiting for someone to pose, so that he could expatiate on it at length and leisure—and which he can now proceed to do. *D'accord* and *évidemment* are not words that Simenon uses much in conversation, but they are somehow implicit in almost every sentence. One has the feeling, listening to his energetic and cordial response to one's questioning, that, like Dr. Johnson, so far as the question of his own writing is concerned, he is delighted 'to concur with the common reader'. From a deep armchair in his study, he expands eloquently on the subject suggested. To write Greek tragedy in terms of life today, '*comme Sophocle, comme Euripide*', exactly (nodding in vigorous agreement), that is exactly what he is trying to do (*précisément . . . évidemment*, etc.). The visitor, by this time himself wonderfully relaxed, has the feeling that at last he is penetrating the essentials.

All this, be it noted, if, but only if, it is a question of the general trends and methods of his work, what has influenced his writing, what he is striving to do, what he believes he has achieved, what he is hoping to achieve in the near future. Once a question about a specific novel is raised, Simenon becomes charmingly and mysteriously vague. Really, he remembers very little about novel 'A'; and in any case he has not re-read it since it appeared: he wrote novel 'B' so long ago and he has written so much since then that he could hardly say anything useful about it. His own favourite? It is always his last. In this case it was *Le Petit Saint*, a book for which—for reasons which will be discussed later and at length—I believe that he has a genuine and affectionate preference.

If it is a question about his life, Simenon bounds happily from his chair and walks up and down the room, mimicking the scene to perfection: the simplicity and innate happiness of his father's character, evinced in his morning walk to the office, sniffing the air, raising his hat; how his first editor at Liège, walking to his office window, taught Simenon to use his eyes as a reporter ('Over there, between St. Nicholas and the Pont Amercoeur, what has appeared on the skyline since last night?'); the way the foreign students, from whom he learned so much, lolled about his mother's kitchen; how, on first arriving in Paris, he used to lie in bed in his attic-bedroom night after night, listening to the hotel tweeny brushing away at innumerable pairs of boots and shoes (this last incident is reproduced faithfully in *Le Passage de la Ligne*, a novel that contains a great deal of Simenon's early experience in Paris).

Watching this performance, I caught myself thinking—what a superb comic actor Simenon would have made! An actor in the *Théâtre du boulevard* tradition—a Louis Jouvet perhaps, not the Jouvet of *Don Juan* and *Le Soulier de Satin*, but the Jouvet of *Knock*. His faithful mimicry seemed a replica of the kind of French comedy that was at its height when he had first arrived in Paris—the comedy, that is to say, that numbered Guitry and Roger-Ferdinand among its playwrights, and had Printemps, Seignier and Valentine Tessier for its enactors. It is a form of comedy that derives directly from the House of Molière, that stable of essential sanity, good-heartedness and human sense of proportion. Indeed, if there is not much that is Molièresque about Simenon's fiction, with the outstanding, even staggering, exception of Maigret himself, there would appear to be a great deal that is Molièresque in his character—not least in his conversation. Embedded in his generous and ready response to all those many and doubtless futile questions that I myself and so many others had posed over the years, there was a glint of that cordial but inevitable *mépris* which the great artist, be he writer or actor, must necessarily feel when confronted by his admirers, however warm, or his critics, however friendly.

In contemporary terms, I got the feeling that Simenon might in some respects be said to resemble one of those Jacques Bonhommes, those bourgeois of wise fantasy, that are such a feature of French seventeenth-century comedy. A man who takes care to dress off-handedly, even rather younger than his years, not out of vanity (who could be vain about check sports jackets or brightly coloured golf pullovers?) but rather out of companionable consideration for the children born to him in middle age; a rich man who believes, as friends of his have told me, that everyone in his household should have the same fare (thus, if the family has lobster for lunch, the whole Epalinges staff—a nanny, cook, two housemaids, two chauffeurs, two secretaries and three gardeners—have lobster too); someone who—and here he is unlike that other writer-millionaire, the late Somerset Maugham, who once remarked that 'Life is too short to do anything for oneself that one can pay others to do for one'—detests waiting for somebody to bring his guest a second bottle of iced lager and prefers to go to the refrigerator and get it himself; a writer who, before beginning a new book, has his whole family medically examined and 'Do Not Disturb—Work In Progress' notices hung up all over the creative part of the house—all this, surely, suggests a manner of life that Molière would have smiled at and commended.

During a pause in this four-hour exchange, he took me on a lightning tour of Epalinges and its surroundings (*'Enfin, l'entr'acte!'*). We visited the power-plant, the swimming-pool, in which his own and numerous other children were splashing one another in happy fury, pretending to play water polo, the bedrooms, the vast kitchen quarters, the nursery, the garden —everything, in fact, but the garage. My host was everywhere at once, opening cupboards and lockers, explaining the innumerable domestic gadgets, exclaiming at his daughter's rows of woolly beasts, his sons' heaped text-books and scholastic etceteras. From a drawer he pulled out and proudly exhibited the wooden block used by his grandfather in the hatter's shop at Liège—

and still used by himself on his own and his children's headgear; Simenon possesses almost as many hats of the felt, canvas and panama variety as he does pipes.

Stunned by the total profusion of his household, the sheer number of persons and things contained in it—and which, to be honest, appeared to surprise him as much as it did me—we returned to the study. At this point Simenon became very confiding. All his life, he explained, he had had the fear of becoming a failure, *un raté*. Not just a plain, common-or-garden failure, a man whose life has fallen into a rut, someone who had misused his talents or his opportunities, but a real sinker, an opter-out of society—a *clochard* on the Paris quais, a 'wino' bum in the Bronx, a 'meth' tramp on the Embankment. This feeling, he went on, was something much more frightening than merely a haunting and abiding fear. A waking nightmare, it was dangerous because it was double-edged, because he knew that in one part of himself there lurked an urge to make just that final act of social oblivion that had hag-ridden his imagination all his life. (This, of course, I reflected sagely if a trifle obviously, is what makes *L'Enterrement de Monsieur Bouvet* such a remarkable book. However, once bitten twice shy: having been faulted so badly already about *Le Président* and other particular items, I wisely kept silent.) Hence, concluded Simenon, smilingly with a wave of his hand, hence all this—Epalinges, the Rolls, the gadgets, the royalties pouring in every ten seconds in more than half the world's currencies. It was all a form of reassurance, a certainty that at this stage of his life he could now never make '*les zones*' or the Bowery. And his furious activity as a writer, I asked tentatively, was that partly accountable to this lifetime obsession? But, of course, (*précisément*)—the one obsession had led to the other.

Shortly afterwards, deeply impressed and having developed, in the space of the afternoon, a great liking for my host, I took my leave. Before I went, he presented me with a copy of one of the rarest of his books—a specially printed edition of *Le Roman de l'Homme*, the text of his famous address delivered at the Brussels Exposition Universelle in 1958. On the fly-leaf he wrote: '*A John Raymond, en attendant de passer sous son scalpel—avec confiance.*' Back in the hotel at Lausanne I read this inscription proudly and gratefully—and yet, I must confess, with a certain mixture of feelings. Certainly, this great artist could face my poor scalpel with confidence. It was rather a question, remembering certain moments of that long and, to me, memorable afternoon's conversation, of whether I could feel equally confident of having escaped un-lethally from his.

Chapter 3

A CHAPTER OF LIMITATIONS

MORE that twenty years ago André Gide told Simenon in a letter that:

> You are living on a false reputation—just like Baudelaire or Chopin. But nothing is more difficult than making the public go back on a too hasty first impression. You are still the slave of your first successes and the reader's idleness would like to put a stop to your triumphs there . . . You are much more *important* than is commonly supposed . . .

Again, in a passage from his *Journal* for 1948, Gide writes:

> Finished *Touriste de Bananes,* one of the least successful novels of Simenon. One is rather vexed with him for this, since in it he spoils a marvellous subject, through haste and, one might say, impatience. Simenon's *subjects* often have a profound psychological and ethical interest. But insufficiently indicated, as if he were not aware of their importance himself, or as if he expected the reader to catch the hint. This is what attracts and holds me in him. He writes for 'the vast public' to be sure, but, delicate and refined readers find something for them too as soon as they deign to take him seriously. He makes one reflect; and this is close to being the height of art; how superior he is in this to those heavy novelists who do not spare us a single commentary! Simenon sets forth a particular fact, perhaps of general interest; but he is careful not to generalize; that is up to the reader.

Taken together, these two extracts furnish a sufficient text on which to hang what one might call a chapter of limitations. They are limitations in two kinds, two opposites. The one arises out of the exuberance and energy of the writer's art, the other is the consequence of his apparent indifference to much that is part of the novelist's working material.

Gide, as we know, was not merely a great admirer of Simenon's fiction, indeed he once planned to write a study of it. He was unashamedly a Simenon-addict—that is to say, he himself belonged to 'the vast public' that he tilts at in the second of these

54

two extracts. Twice in the last volume of his *Journal* he plainly admits to this addiction—for example, when he writes, sometime in 1944, that he has 'just devoured one after another of eight books by Simenon at the rate of one a day (this was the second reading for *Long Cours, Les Inconnus dans la Maison* and *Le Pendu de Saint-Pholien*)' and again, four years later, when he notes that he has taken 'a new plunge into Simenon; I have just read six in a row'. This, surely, is the way in which an addict does read a writer that he not only admires but one could almost say physically enjoys reading. And undoubtedly, with the exception of the long fictional centre-pieces, such as *Le Voyageur de la Toussaint, Lettre à mon Juge, Le Testament Donadieu, L'Aîné des Ferchaux* and *La Neige était sale*, and the group of novels written during the last five years, *Le Petit Saint, La Mort d'Auguste* and *Le Chat*, this 'plunge' method is the ideal way in which to read Simenon—certainly the right way to obtain the greatest measure of enjoyment from the Maigret series. All this is not to say that Gide, the pre-eminent and prehensile stylist, was unaware of Simenon's own ambitions and attainments in this respect. The earliest mention of his work in the *Journal* occurs when Gide notes his pleasure at the use of the verb *divaguer* in *Pietr-le-Letton*: '*Il divaguait dans les coulisses de l'hôtel.*'

The two criticisms quoted above are obviously not made from the same angle. The first is external, a warning addressed to the writer against allowing himself to be influenced or limited by his public. Such exhortations (*Excelsior!*) spring more or less directly from the creed of Flaubert—Art, in this case specifically the Novel, for its own sake; away with those first successes and public triumphs that put a full-stop to the artist's development! It is ironic to reflect that, in an earlier and a less self-conscious Age of the Novel, it was the very opposite fear—namely, that the reader, far from being idle, would grow bored with repeat-performances —that urged the writer on to strike new imaginative ground. Thus, for instance, Sir Walter Scott writes in the introduction to the 1830 edition of *Ivanhoe* that: 'Nothing can be more dangerous for the fame of a professor of the fine arts, than to permit (if he can possibly prevent it) the character of a mannerist to be attached to him or that he should be supposed capable of success only in a

particular or limited style. The public are, in general, very ready
to adopt the opinion, that he who has pleased them in one
particular mode of composition, is, by means of that very talent,
rendered incapable of venturing upon other subjects.' Scott
was, of course, speaking of a purely horizontal transition from
'Scottish manners, Scottish dialect, and Scottish characters of
note' to the making use of similar or equivalent material across
the Border. Yet, to judge by the range and the variety in depth
of his countless canvases, it almost seems as if Simenon had shown
himself more attentive to Sir Walter's maxims than to Gide's
strictures—or rather, perhaps, that, after his Simenon-Sim,
Janus-faced fashion, he has been faithful to both. Certainly, it is
fair to assert that had Gide lived to read some of his friend's
later productions, he would have been bound to admit that the
Flaubertian *Excelsior!* had not been altogether abandoned.

Personally, I am inclined to believe that when Gide speaks of
Simenon as being the slave of his public and of his first successes,
he fails to reach the heart of the matter—that *le cas Simenon*
is more complicated and more unavoidable than he thinks. The
fact is that for much of his mature writing life, Simenon has been
the slave of his daemon, his furious and ceaseless creative activity
—an activity that owes nothing to his readers' demands on him
or to his being a public artist-serf but is the plain consequence
of his statement that 'If I were to cease writing, I should die'.
As the total volume of his work insists, this is no empty rhetoric
but a simple declaration of fact. (Sarah Bernhardt, as great an
artist in her own line of energy as Simenon in his, may have
sounded more rhetorical but she was just as sincere when she
told Queen Mary after her last Command Performance: 'Madame,
I shall die upon the stage! It is my battlefield!') Like all great
romantic imaginations—Balzac, Hugo, Dickens, Scott himself,
or, in their own business of the theatre, Bernhardt, Irving or
Olivier—Simenon has sometimes seemed to betray his art or
rather to fall below the height of his powers as a writer, when in
fact he is merely the unconscious victim of his own Achilles heel.
Such victimization is the penalty of genius—nor, except in a
minuscule age like the present, should we need to be reminded
that as far as the art of fiction is concerned, the primary symbol

in the algebraical equation of genius of this kind is energy. This over-plus of energy takes as many forms, produces as many varieties of the Achilles heel, as there are novelists of genius. Thus Balzac often tires his reader with bogus theosophy or tenth-rate melodrama (*La Recherche de l'Absolu*, *César Birotteau*, etc.); Hugo drenches him with Channel sea-spray (*Les Travailleurs de la Mer*) or plagues him with gaseous philosophizing about human nature (*Les Misérables*); Dickens pours buckets of tears over him, Scott shuts him up in suits of armour and so on.

Simenon's Achilles heel, at least for my money, is his tendency to indulge in a kind of arch black comedy for its own arch sake, gargoylish hobbledehoy humour, a repetition of noises intended to startle the reader like the striking of a sadistic cuckoo clock—all this together with a note of plaintive down-and-out whimsy that one remembers as a feature of poorish French film comedies in the Thirties; the whole *Kitsch* caboodle could, in fact, be described as a combination of bad German Ufa and bad Fernandel film scenarios. None of this derives from the demands of Simenon's public, though, as we know, some of his most popular novels contain the grossest instances of these divagations into cuckoo clock machinery: it is, one suspects, the marginal product of his provincialism and of his early ambition to be a kind of mock-Gothic humorist.

Fortunately for his readers and for Simenon himself, these unattractive traits occur only in specific books: they do not affect his work as a whole, but come out all over one or two of his novels, including some of the early Maigrets, in a rash, as it were, doing little or no harm to the rest of his fiction. To give two flagrant examples—two of his greatest public successes, later successfully filmed—I would instance *Monsieur La Souris* and the even better-known *L'Homme qui regardait passer les trains*, both published in 1938, a year that saw no less than twelve new Simenon titles appearing on the bookstalls.

The first concerns a little old Paris tramp named Mosselbach, alias the Mouse, who finds a stack of dollar bills on the body of a dead man discovered in a car off the Champs-Elysées. For those who have developed a kind of Sherlock Holmes Society attitude towards Maigret, it will have been noted that the book marks the appearance of Lognon, the tireless, lugubrious Paris police inspector who figures as the hero-victim of *Maigret et le Fantôme*. *Monsieur La Souris* is largely a kind of step-by-step comic duel between Lognon and the Mouse, the one stalking the other to and fro across Paris in an endeavour to unravel the truth about the murdered man. As a film treatment the book would undoubtedly succeed; as a novel, it only succeeds in irritating. Ironically, the one effective figure in this ponderous farce (or *sotie*, as Gide, with his own *Les Caves du Vatican* in mind, would probably have preferred to call it) is Herr Martin Oosting of Basle, the international banker-tycoon and type of power-merchant who would have interested Balzac, or, for that matter, Zola, but who merely bores Simenon:

> Martin Oosting had tackled the matter at the top. He was a man with stubbly grey hair and black clothes hanging loosely over a fat, heavy body. From morning to night he smoked cigars without bothering whether the smoke blew into the faces of the people to whom he was talking.
>
> If he had ever laughed, it must have been years before, during his childhood. When he entered a room, a sombre look in his eyes, crushing the floor beneath his heavy steps, it was impossible not to understand that he was the most important person present.
>
> At the Hôtel du Louvre, everybody had realized that straight away, as soon as he got out of his taxi, when, without a word, with a categorical and almost threatening gesture, he had prevented the commissionaire from taking the little suitcase he was holding.
>
> He had made for the reception desk and, looking down at the young man in tails behind it, he had growled: 'Martin Oosting.'
>
> For, of course, he had had a suite reserved for him. There was already a whole pile of telegrams waiting for him. Still standing, he ripped them open with one fingernail, and read them as if his gaze had been capable of crushing the letters on the paper.

From his hotel suite he dictates a press communiqué on his colleague's murder:

> . . . *that it is regrettable that it should have been thought fit to give indecent publicity to certain details of his private life which have not even been proved* . . .
>
> Behind these words could be discerned the huge old-fashioned edifice of the C.M.B., in which for the past two centuries men as massive as Oosting or the carved furniture had gathered together in the council chamber, paved with black and white marble, and quietly, in an almost cathedral-like whisper, had organized colossal schemes.

It is the kind of satirical thumbnail sketch that the disinterested Sim, *doppelgänger* and Slave of the Lamp, can achieve with his eyes shut for the advancement of Simenon's fantasy, but in the context of the Mouse's heavy drollery it makes for genuine relief.

L'Homme qui regardait passer les trains is an altogether more ambitious affair. When Kees Popinga, an upright citizen in his late thirties, a model husband and father, an avid chess player, the managing clerk of Groningen's leading firm of ship's chandlers, learns that his firm is bankrupt, he goes berserk. He rapes and murders his ex-employer's mistress in an Amsterdam hotel and entrains for Paris where he leads the police a mountingly boastful game of hide-and-seek, ending up cheerfully in a Dutch asylum:

> Only this wasn't the Groningen chess club, nor a Paris café, and on the table were only cups of tea. Nevertheless, noticing a bishop threatening him, Kees simply couldn't help whisking it away, while fingering another chessman to divert attention, and dropping it into his teacup, as formerly he'd dropped Copenghem's bishop into a tankard of beer.
>
> For a moment the doctor could not imagine what had happened; then he caught sight of the chessman in the cup and rose hastily to his feet.
>
> 'Afraid I must ask you to excuse me. I've just remembered an appointment.'
>
> Naturally! He hadn't realized that Kees had done it deliberately. Yet why should he have denied himself the pleasure of recalling an incident of the old days?
>
> 'And *I* must ask you to excuse *me*,' Kees said politely. 'It's an old story, and would take too long explaining. And in any case you wouldn't understand.'
>
> It couldn't be helped, and anyhow it was safer thus. Which was confirmed by the fact that next day the doctor requested Kees to produce the exercise-book in which he was supposed to be writing his memoirs. There was nothing but the title:
>
> THE TRUTH
> ABOUT THE KEES POPINGA CASE
>
> The doctor looked up in surprise, evidently wondering why his patient had written no more. And Kees felt called on to explain, with a rather forced smile:
>
> 'Really, there isn't any truth about it, is there, doctor?'

Despite all the impressive tributes that have been paid this novel, that last sentence describes it as a whole with deadly accuracy. Far from its being a profound study of a paranoiac and its hero an adumbration of the Dostoevskyan psychopath, the book is a brilliant and totally unreal invention from start to finish. Its basic situation—that of the earning man of property who goes off the rails once his economic status collapses—might be described as neo-Marxist, since it is one dear to the masochistic side of the bourgeois imagination; in terms of the West End matinée theatre of the 1920s, and '30s, for example, it is the theme of Maugham's *The Breadwinner*. In Simenon's hands, the book is a pure exercise in macabre fantasy. The men and women whom Popinga encounters while on the run—the tarts and gangsters, his sardonic ex-employer, the tireless police sleuth Lucas—are scant but real enough. Popinga himself is merely a Grand Guignol puppet of his creator's over-plus imagination. It is consoling to reflect that just as Simenon got rid of most of his whimsical streak in *Monsieur La Souris*, so he spent this fake clinical fantasy side of his imagination in the same year—a year which also witnessed the genuine and touching comedy of *La Marie du Port*, one of the writer's rare penetrations into a world of old-fashioned sentiment, and the remarkable *Les Rescapés du 'Télémaque'*, itself the precursor of the great realistic *romans d'aventure* that are the central feature of Simenon's middle period. The great merit of *L'Homme qui regardait passer les trains* is negative and twofold: first, because, like a false stone, it serves to set off the real jewels in the Simenon collection in their proper lustre; secondly, because it prompts the reader to reflect upon the real psychopathology of everyday life as it exists in the world of Simenon's imagination. One has only to compare Kees Popinga with Alavoine or Gobillot, with the Paris widower, the Levantine lodger at Charleroi or even the hatter and mass-murderer of La Rochelle, to see that in this strange but compelling assortment of characters and destinies Kees is the joker in the pack. In contrast to these more or less average human beings driven by circumstances, and the Kindly Ones, to their most un-average conclusions, he is an artificial construction. He has no identity, no imaginative reality, beyond the cleverness of his creator's picaresque contriving.

★

So much for the limitations of exuberance. The limitations imposed by Simenon's apparent indifference—to ambition, fame, the power and the glory (sacred, profane or merely secular), religious insight, political endeavour, acts of impersonal will or cerebration—all this presents a problem far more difficult to determine. Since the hint of it is to be found in the second of Gide's criticisms, his comments on *Touriste de Bananes*, it seems necessary to ask ourselves, first, what that extraordinary novel is really about and secondly, what part of its essential content is, in Gide's opinion, 'insufficiently indicated'.

The phrase 'banana tourist' is a local expression of contempt for those who dream of living the simple life of nature in the South Sea Islands. Here it is applied to Oscar Donadieu, the youngest son of La Rochelle's leading shipowner, whose mysterious death, falling off a wharf one night into the harbour, and the family's subsequent scandals and bankruptcy is the theme of *Le Testament Donadieu* (1937). Oscar, the gangling, reserved, teen-aged 'Kiki' in the earlier book, is now twenty-five and 'as shy and awkward as he had been at half that age'. Strictly, he is not a banana tourist:

> . . . He was not the weakling, the drifter, they supposed. He knew that he was following, had followed all his life long, not the line of least resistance, but a definite ideal. As a boy, in the family mansion at La Rochelle, he had been looked down on because he was 'backward' and without initiative; yet one November Sunday afternoon he had made his way cross-country almost to Sables d'Olonne, where he intended to ship on the first boat he saw as cabin-boy or deck-hand.
>
> When the family became involved in financial and domestic complications of a more or less unsavoury order, had he not made his escape again, after his fashion, by spending long hours on gymnastic exercises, under his tutor's guidance, and vanquishing his physical weakness; with the result that now he was tall and muscular above the average of his generation?
>
> Then, disgusted by the sight of his sisters and brothers-in-law squabbling over his dead father's estate, he had fled once more—this time to America—and joined the host of workers, of all nationalities, employed on a great dam. There, again, he had to struggle with a physical infirmity, his fear of heights, and he had fought it down so successfully that, at the end, he could work for hours on the highest scaffolding with hardly a trace of dizziness.

> . . . All his life there had been something for him to fight down:
> his physical weakness, as a child; his fear of heights, when he was
> working on the dam; and, more recently, his disgust when he had
> found himself involved, much against his will, in the family
> catastrophe. It was nothing new for him, this sense that he must
> struggle to keep his end up.
> But why was there never anyone to talk to him in his own language,
> and to understand at least, even if he could not share, his aspirations?
> . . . All he desired was to escape from the herd, to lead a simple
> but laborious life, digging the soil, and learning to spear fish, as the
> natives did, in the lagoon . . .

Oscar's disenchantment—not with the life of nature, though
that, too, sports with him mercilessly during his six months'
solitude in the island valley, but with life itself and the crapulous
colonial half-world that surrounds him—builds up to a horrific
climax. Certainly, there would seem to be no 'insufficiency' in
this direction. The book's secondary theme not only precipitates
young Donadieu's individual fate but quite simply engulfs and
takes over the novel itself. It concerns the arrest and trial of
Ferdinand Lagre, the merchant ship's captain whose infatuation
for Tamatéa, a Tahitian prostitute, has led him to murder one of
his own ship's officers. Tamatéa is an 'amateur' in the sense that
she sleeps around for money and drinks, or out of plain camaraderie
among her own set in the sleazy *Relai des Méridiens* whose owner,
the nauseous fever-stricken Manière, with his 'greasy hair with a
parting down the middle' and 'big grey-green red-rimmed eyes,
with something almost sinister in their expression', is one of a
long line of maleficent proprietors and bar-tenders ministering to
Simenon's own brand of tropical Limbo. Sitting in the *Relai*, after
Lagre has been sentenced, following a rigged trial, to a term of
imprisonment agreed on beforehand by the judge, the prosecution
and his own counsel at Government House, Donadieu waits for
his companions:

> . . . while he believed himself to be thinking about something
> quite different, a word came back to his memory, one he hadn't
> heard for years, the word 'Limbo'.
> What was that bit about it in the Catechism?
> 'The souls of infants who die before they have received the
> Sacrament of baptism dwell for a certain time in Limbo.' And it struck
> him that this shabby, dreary restaurant, where the three of them

sat stolidly waiting, with mosquitoes droning in the languid air, resembled his conception of Limbo: as a sort of grey expanse of emptiness, where life was in abeyance, nothing stirred.

Simenon's Limbo is worse than anything to be found in Graham Greene's tropics, since it has no saving clauses or theological life-lines attached. Just as each Simenonian world, whatever the climate, is solipsistic, so each of his tragic characters is imprisoned in his own solitude, vainly striving to break through the opaque cloud of unknowing and misunderstanding that separates all human beings. It is this acute and egoistic sense of his own alienation that leads Donadieu to rivet his mind and feelings on the fate of Captain Lagre, formerly an officer in the Donadieu employ:

> ... He had an absurd impression ... that he was failing in respect towards the man whose life was at stake and at whom he hardly dared to look.
> 'He seems quite flattened out,' the lawyer had said. 'As if he'd lost his wits altogether.'
> Donadieu, however, felt sure that this was not the case, and he kept trying to understand, to put himself in the place of the man standing there, only a few feet in front of him, isolated from the outside world not so much by the rails of the dock as by a barrier of incomprehension.
> For, when all was said and done, it was he, and he only, who had killed a fellow-man. He alone could know what it really meant, and how little to the point were all these tedious formalities and long-winded phrases.

His knowledge of Lagre's plight and what lies behind it increases his feeling of a division, not only between himself and the rest of the world, but of a deep split within his own personality:

> ... he realized exactly what he should have done, and pictured himself, the real Donadieu, rising from his seat, pale with indignation, flinging his challenge at these callous brutes.
> 'Is it your idea of French justice that, while a case is under trial, the Judge should go and lunch with the Governor and try to find out his wishes as to the verdict? Is it the right thing for the defending counsel to hobnob with the Prosecutor over coffee and liqueurs? And can you explain why the presence of the prisoner's wife—whom you refer to as "that damned old woman"—should be thought undesirable? Poor Madame Lagre has crossed two oceans to come to her husband's aid. And now you want to exclude her from this trial, in which her husband's liberty, perhaps his life, is at stake!'

. . . He should have taken a taxi and, by now, been at the Hôtel des Iles, saying:

'I'm young Donadieu. And I'm your son's godfather, as you may remember. It so happens that I know all the dirty work that's going on behind the scenes in connection with this trial. At this very moment they're sitting round a table at Government House, swilling drinks and fixing up between them what the sentence is to be. Your lawyer's letting you down; he's going there too, to get his orders. He isn't even trying to defend his client. It's for you to make a protest and insist on a proper trial while there's still time . . .'

By implication, *Touriste de Bananes* is one of the fiercest indictments of colonial bureaucracy that has ever been written. The total separation of appearance and reality culminates in the brutal farce of the trial: here the examination of Tamatéa by the elderly libidinous Judge Isnard owes its ironic point to the fact that, until the pair were discovered *in flagrante* by Mme. Isnard, the Judge had himself been keeping the girl—a fact known to the whole community, from the cynical, easy-going Governor downwards. Candé, the Chief Secretary, is a man of a mysterious and unsavoury background; the probity and innate decency of Beaudoin, Lagre's defence counsel, has been anaesthetized and destroyed by drink, womanising and the climate to such an extent that he has become a fixer, like the rest of them—though, as his contacts with Donadieu reveal, a fixer with remorseful moments. (Needless to say, remorse and never repentance is the abiding characteristic of all Simenon's moral defaulters.) The atmosphere of the Colonial Club—where the Judge, baulked of Tamatéa, always contrives to leave last in the evenings so as to have a drab and furtive tumble with Mme. Bon, the club's ageing housekeeper —compares interestingly with Collector Turton's conformist circle at Chandrapore in *A Passage to India*. Here, at least, the perfidious Raj and its hypocritical code has the edge in maintaining standards. Though the actual indictment is put into Donadieu's mouth or, rather, into his thought-stream, the whole book is a powerful reminder that however admirably the French have disseminated their civilization, they themselves do, or did, not export well as bureaucrats. (Those who doubt the truthful background of Simenon's picture should consult Walter G. Langrois's *André Malraux: The Indochina Adventure*, an admirably depressive and documented study of judicial miscarriage and politico-financial 'fixing' in one of the largest dependencies of the French Empire between the wars.) It is hard to see how Gide, himself such a powerful castigator of colonialism in his *Voyage au Congo* (1929), could feel that this general *mise-en-scène* had been 'insufficiently indicated'.

What, then, has been left out of the novel, what ends, ethical or psychological, have not been pursued, explored or followed through by Simenon—whether out of impatience or for other reasons? I confess that I can only think of two aspects that might, at least to Gide's satisfaction, have been further developed. One is purely psychological, the other arises out of what, for want of a better expression, I would tentatively and provisionally term psychological rhetoric. By this I mean the kind of psychology that belongs to or exists in the imagination—as it were, in literature proper. It has, of course, no scientific validity. It would make little appeal to a pupil of Dr. Rycroft or Professor Sprott and none at all to a pupil of Professor Eysenck's. In terms of the novel it is simply the method by which a writer builds up a moral image of character in the reader's mind—an image that persists whether the character himself emerges triumphantly from circumstances or is undermined by them. Such 'prestige' characters are generally the creation of writers in whom an intense moral imagination and a certain density of style are conjoined. Heyst in *Victory* is exactly a type of the character I have in mind. Indeed, Simenon's stoical but infatuated Captain Lagre would, in the hands of Conrad, assume heroic proportions of a sort which Gide —a fervent admirer of Conrad and himself the creator of the heroic and Jansenistic Alissa in *La Porte Etroite*—would be the first to appreciate. Could the projection of Lagre's character—his essential nobility and tragic destiny set against the human larvae of the island's White Community, bent on his destruction—be Simenon's missing equation? His admiration for Conrad's fiction is as great as Gide's own and in at least one of his novels (as we shall see in Chapter 5) he *has* created a character that might, in his own terms, be described as genuinely and legitimately Conradian in conception. But he has certainly not done so here. To do so, he would have to be, in terms of his own psychology and, even more, of his own technique, an entirely different and a far less original writer.

As I see it, the only clue that its author has failed to follow up in *Touriste de Bananes* is that which is disclosed in the nature of Oscar Donadieu himself. For all his fierce disclaimers, Simenon is a moralist in the central French tradition and however obsessed with the misery of the human situation, his brief demands that he take certain necessary, even ugly truths about the human heart into account. As one burdened with this knowledge and writing in this tradition, *Touriste de Bananes* may be said to pose the question, psychological or ethical, of how much our anxiety and concern for the fate of others stems from the feeling of isolation in ourselves. How much of Donadieu's indignation on behalf of Lagre is the outcome of his own self-pity—a self-pity that results in the novel ending with the discovery of his suicide? This certainly is a psychological situation Simenon does leave unresolved or rather, in Gide's phrase, leaves the reader to reflect upon for himself.

Chapter 4

CROSS-EXAMINATION

As I said at the beginning, this short study is merely an interim and explanatory dossier. If it helps to serve public notice of an achievement far greater than Simenon's average readers have realized or perhaps supposed even, it will have achieved its purpose and the writer will have done what he set out to do. In this chapter I propose, among other things, to call my witness-in-chief, leaving the cross-examination in the tried hands of M. Parinaud. However much one differs from Parinaud's conclusions, his knowledge of and devotion to Simenon's work surpasses that of most of his critics. Some twelve years ago he interviewed his subject extensively on the Radiodiffusion Française, eliciting the fullest and most revealing account of the writer's aims and methods that had so far been vouchsafed. The fact that so much contained in this interesting document still stands is, I believe, mainly due to Parinaud's obstinate persistence as an interrogator. Meanwhile, before attempting a paraphrase of their conversation and commenting upon it, we shall indulge in a brief digression. On the threshold of entering Simenon's dark and ambiguous territory, it might be as well to consult a few familiar and less Delphic oracles.

In an appendix to his *Critical Readings in the Modern French Novel*, Professor Cruickshank recently reproduced a number of general remarks concerning the craft of fiction made by some dozen distinguished practitioners from Romain Rolland to Michel Butor. Needless to say (or strangely enough, according to one's view of the academic temperament), Simenon, though he has made many off-the-cuff statements about his work from time to time, was not included in this professorial *catena*. Yet if we apply a few of these magisterial pronouncements and random observations to his work, eliminating whatever opinions are alien or of no

67

concern to it, and emphasizing the points at which their theory coincides with his practice, we may be enabled to form a clearer idea of Simenon's own aims and methods as a writer. By ranging these professional dicta alongside the body of his work, we can at least obtain a fair idea of what he is *not* setting out to achieve as a novelist. When a writer has written so much and in such an apparent variety of manners, such comparative and negative conclusions can be extremely useful. They not only help to clear the ground for a positive assessment but, by doing so, assist the reader to a keener differentiation within the material of the work itself. By defining the autonomous boundaries of Simenon's imagination, the way in which his artistic purposes differ or diverge from those of his fellow-novelists, we are in a better position to appreciate its confederate nature. The lion and the fox in his genius—or rather, the pride of lions and the ubiquitous complement of foxes —can be the more clearly distinguished.

At the outset we are partially rewarded. The professor's initial witness is (of all people!) Romain Rolland. He gives an account of his original conception of the novel he is about to write which corresponds, at least to begin with, to Simenon's own account of the way in which a novel first shapes itself in his imagination. The idea comes to him (so Rolland told Jean Bonnerot in a letter written in 1909) in the form of a musical impression—a nebula that radiates, since Rolland was a ponderous, meticulous planner of long-winded novels, given to double tetralogies and pentalogies, down through each volume of the series to the individual chapters and, so he claims, even paragraphs. For Simenon, whose general aim is to get his work completed (and sometimes, as both Gide and Miss Brophy have legitimately complained, less than completed) in the space of between 200 and 250 pages, it is the musical phrase or mood that registers in his mind at the very beginning of a new work and safely takes charge of it thereafter. Before the basic character or protagonist has been even vaguely imagined, and long before the telephone directories have been ransacked, the manila dossier been opened or the street maps examined— it is this phrase of feeling in which the whole unknown drama is to be couched, that sets his imagination working.

From Rolland to Gide—preoccupied, as always, with the

question of artistic form. What a free, what a 'lawless' form the novel is, muses Edouard in *Les Faux Monnayeurs*. Yet all these novelists, sighing for artistic freedom of expression, how they all panic when they get it! How they chain themselves to reality, the English and the Russians as much as the French. What literature, after all, is as genuinely human as Greek or French seventeenth-century tragedy—those masterpieces whose perfection, whose profound humanity even, have only been achieved by deliberate withdrawal from the kind of surface real-life that the would-be naturalists are bent on hitting off. And so on and so on. To all this one imagines that Simenon would not have much to say. For us, his readers, there are two points worth taking up. The first concerns 'reality', 'realism' and the presentation of 'real life' in the novel. For our purpose of appreciating and defining the nature and extent of his art, Simenon may be said to be a novelist writing in mixed modes. In this sense he is true first cousin to Balzac. For such a writer terms like 'realism' and 'real life' have an ambiguous meaning that would be lost on a perfectionist of the *irréel* such as Gide, whose bracketing of Greek and French tragedy argues a psychological insensibility towards the first that seems extraordinary in one who prided himself on his catholic appreciation of literature as a whole and his un-French appetite for the irrational.

There follow two extracts from Proust, both taken from the long creative meditation in the second part of *Le Temps retrouvé*. The first states the plain but painful truth obvious to every un-self-indulgent writer—namely, that a work of art that is cluttered with theories, psychological, political, socio-scientific or whatever, is like a gift on which the price tag remains, and a diminishing price tag at that. Since Simenon's work is blessedly free from theories of every kind (too much so in some critical opinions), this caution does not apply. The professor's second extract concerns the interchangeableness of imagination and sensibility. Marcel, the narrator, asks himself whether

> . . . in the creation of a literary work the imagination and the sensibility are not interchangeable and whether the second, without disadvantage, cannot be substituted for the first just as people whose stomach is incapable of digesting entrust this function to their

intestines. An innately sensitive man who has no imagination could, nevertheless, write admirable novels. The suffering caused him by others and the conflict provoked by his efforts to protect himself against them, such experiences interpreted by the intelligence might provide material for a book as beautiful as if it were imagined and invented and as objective, as startling and unexpected as the author's imaginative fancy would have been had he been happy and free from persecution.

A large and debatable subject but one which hardly affects the basic methods of Simenon's story-telling, which necessarily entail the use of both qualities since, in the terms of his art, neither imagination nor sensibility can act as a substitute for one another without spoiling the balance of the whole. Unlike the kind of novelist whom Proust postulates in this passage, Simenon is no free agent. His art, like the art of Stevenson, Conrad and Graham Greene, is rooted in the telling of a story. He must, like them, abide by the narrative question. If, because of a defect in sensibility and an over-concentration on plot, the imaginative narrative occasionally seems to fall flat—as happens, for example, in that celebrated early Maigret, *La Nuit du Carrefour* (1932)—a display of psychological sensibility in the void (I am thinking here of *Le Temps d'Anaïs*, 1951) leaves the reader with an impression of shamanic hocus-pocus. The poor wretch of a protagonist is dissolved in the super-impressive personality of his analyst and, as the novel progresses, it reads more and more like the reconstruction of case data recorded in a hero-worshipping student's notebook.

Mauriac's remarks on the art of fiction are impeccable and sagely banal. Life, he reminds us, is the novelist's point of departure, it is art that enables him to make life swerve and change direction, turning what is hidden into effective action, reversing the roles of men and women, finding the executioner in the victim and vice versa. To all this Simenon would easily assent. Indeed, as far as the victim and the executioner are concerned, he has put it in his own terms in the mind of Emile, the victimized would-be murderer of *Dimanche*. 'If one is satisfied with over-simple explanations,' Emile meditates,

> . . . one ends by reasoning like the newspapers which state:
> *Because he was drunk, a lock-keeper has hacked his wife to death with a knife.*

Why was he drunk? And why a knife? Why his wife? Above all, why does nobody ask why she was not a natural victim?

For if one admits the criminal type of a murderer, one may suppose there is also the type of the natural victim, all of which leads to the conclusion that, in crime, the man or woman killed deserved to be called to account quite as much as the man or woman who did the killing.

Similarly, Mauriac's rather unctuous claim, made in his *Vie de Jésus,* and out of Professor Cruickshank's context, to 'know himself, if he may say so, in heroes of his own invention', might be Simenon's own, though made without the sugary overtones of Saint-Sulpice.

Bernanos's assertion that God and the Devil are indispensable to the novelist, and that 'naturalism' only turns the difficulty by transforming man into a beast, cuts no ice with Simenon, to the majority of whose characters the news that God is dead is as stale as it was startling when first communicated to Nietzsche's Zarathustra. There are few enough *faux dévots,* let alone genuine religiously-minded human-beings in his repertoire. What is more important, as a consequence of God's being dead, Simenon's work contains very little positive evil, using the word in a theological sense. (The great exception to this apparent paradox is *La Neige était sale.*) As for 'naturalism' transforming men into mere beasts, this may be true in extreme cases—such as Zola's *La Terre,* for example—but it is quite irrelevant to Simenon's tragedies. There are tramps, cretins, vagrants, psychopaths galore in his pages, particularly in his scenes of peasant life (old Couderc in *La Veuve Couderc,* the epileptic son-in-law in *Le Haut Mal,* Cottin in *Le Rapport du Gendarme* and so on). Yet humanity as a whole is never brutalized and transformed. It may indeed be stratified and divided up, in its creator's unusual and, indeed, entirely original manner, for Simenon, as we shall shortly see, has his own Elect as he also has his vast and inclusive category of Untouchables. In any case, Bernanos's theological tug-of-war games find no place in his fiction.

Malraux, like Mauriac, merely proffers a professional bromide. The value of a novel, he tells us sententiously, lies not in the degree of passion or detachment that inspires it but in the harmony that exists between the subject expressed and the means employed to express it. Sartre, as one would expect, is stimulating and combative. The novelist, he declares roundly, shuns the world he lives in on pain of treason and bad faith; it was made for him and he for it, it is '*sa chance unique*'. For this reason we must regret Balzac's indifference to the events of July '48 and Flaubert's total misunderstanding of the Commune. Regret it for *their* sakes since it represents something in their work that is lost to it and will be for ever lacking. Perhaps our own historical patch of time is a poor thing, but it is our own; we have nothing but this life to live, in the midst of this war or that revolution. For a writer to remain dumb in face of his contemporary situation is not only cowardice but constitutes in itself a form of action, since not only does each word have its echoes but each silence also. The novelist who spends his life writing tales of a Hittite civilization may himself be said to have taken up a position. And Sartre concludes his procureur-général's speech by stating that he holds Flaubert and the surviving Goncourt brother responsible for the repression that followed the Commune, because neither of them had written a line to prevent it.

This is strong if predictable stuff. Where, we wonder, does Simenon stand in relation to this doctrine of contemporary commital? In the public quasi-historical sense adduced by Sartre, the answer must surely be 'nowhere'. Simenon has his own form of committal but it is not committal to the contemporary situation.

No one, Simenon least of all, would quarrel with Simone de Beauvoir's assertion that the novel is a unique and irreducible form of communicating human experience—the kind of experience that cannot be contained in the essay or the work of philosophy. Camus's contention that the novelist's world may be considered a 'correction' of real life, following a preferred inner line ('*le désir profond de l'Homme*'), would seem to run parallel to Simenon's conception of it as man's life pushed to its imaginative extremities. In connection with Camus it is interesting to note that the symbolic claims made for *La Peste*—that it contains 'typological ironies', with Oran standing for a historical community ('France, for example, on the eve of the Occupation')—have recently been made, in much the same applied sense, for *Le Train*. If this were really so, Simenon would merit inclusion among the Sartreans who, unlike Balzac, Flaubert and Goncourt, have not by-passed their contemporary situation. Alas, whatever their value for Camus, situational ironies of this kind are not for Simenon, and certainly not for Sim, that canny jobbing builder, whose budget would never run to them. Simenon, Sim et Cie may have made use of the fall of France as the background for human drama but any larger historically symbolic intentions on the firm's part are non-existent.

Lastly, Robbe-Grillet, for whom 'the novel is neither significant nor absurd. It *is*, *tout simplement*', etc.—only interesting here because his pretentious experimental type of fiction, in which the novel, freed 'from sheer temporality, sheer causality, falsely certain description, clear story', moves forward 'without reference to real time', has been described as a method of refining 'upon certain sophisticated conventions developed by Simenon in the Maigret novels'. It is a relief to note that Mr. Frank Kermode, the original discoverer of this affinity, adds that in them (the Maigret books) 'the dark side of the plot is eventually given a reasonable explanation, whereas in Robbe-Grillet the need for this has gone'.

What, in relation to Simenon, do we make of these pronouncements? That, like Romain Rolland, he begins a novel from a phrase of music and that this phrase pitches the key and determines the mood of the drama that is to follow; that he writes, like Balzac, in a 'mixed mode' of realism and romanticism to an extent that his critics and admirers will continue, other things being equal, to argue, as they did in the case of Balzac, as to whether he is primarily an exponent of one or the other—whereas it is our contention that each of Simenon's novels is in some sense a hybrid mixture or, more accurately, a chemical compound of realistic and romanesque elements, whose formula varies in each case according to the prevailing creative phrase or mood; that his dramas have a psychic irrationality that is consistent with Simenon's own artistic vision of life and owes little or nothing to formal literary psychology using that phrase in the sense that is meant by our saying that the sexual feelings of *Phèdre*, for example, or the pattern of *gloire* that we trace in the drama of Corneille constitutes a formal or 'straight' psychology

of the passions; and to this we would add, making the same
distinction as before, that Simenon's tragedies, by virtue of their
irrationality, their consistent concern with plot and peripeteia,
do bear a profound thematic resemblance to that very different
kind of tragedy composed by the Greek dramatists—a tragedy
ultimately founded on the cohesive, if not always coherent,
irrationality of myth.

Proceeding in the wake of Professor Cruickshank's cloud of
witnesses, we merely note that Simenon's art is purged of theory
(as if, indeed, it ever needed purging!) and that, in his case at
least, sensibility can never be a substitute for imagination, since
his first aim is to tell a story or, as the experts put it, construct a
fictional paradigm. Such searching for a story must obviously
begin in the midst of real life, as Mauriac recommends, and
must just as obviously entail a departure from it, turning off at
some point in the main high road of 'reality' to follow its own
pathway towards an implicit yet undiscovered end. And here,
bearing 'in the midst' in mind and remembering the consummate
and devilish use of time that Simenon employs in his novels,
one is tempted to pause and consider how, in quite another
connection, a recipe from Sir Philip Sidney finds an echo in his
fictional constructions. 'A poet,' Sidney writes, 'thrusteth into
the middest, euen where it most concerneth him, and there
recoursing to the thinges forepaste, and diuining of thinges to
come, maketh a pleasing analysis of all.' It is a method that
Simenon has made use of on many of his most successful
occasions.

As we have seen, his universe contains neither God nor the
Devil. This, while it leaves most of his assembled repertoire
joyless and partly living, never denies to his most effective men
and women their passionate intensity or, as Bernanos would
suggest, degrades the majority to a state of aimless brutishness.
As he explained to Parinaud a long time ago, Simenon has never
had much belief in active happiness, feeling that it exists most
recognizably as a state of equilibrium, more or less stable at
various moments in our lives. In any case it would be fair to say
that Simenon *qua* novelist, like Proust in the same long meditation
quoted earlier, believes that 'those who pose for happiness are

not, as a rule, able to spare us many sittings'. To which one would add, in Simenon's case as in Proust's, the painful corollary that

> . . . those who pose to us for sorrow give us plenty of sittings in the studio we only use at those periods. That studio is within ourselves. Those periods are a picture of our life with its diverse sufferings. For they contain others, and just when we think we are calm, a new one is born, new in all senses of the word; perhaps because unforeseen situations force us to enter into deeper contact with ourselves, the painful dilemmas in which love places us at every instant, instruct us, disclose to us successively the matter of which we are made.

Thus, with Sartre and Camus answered, Mme. de Beauvoir agreed with and Robbe-Grillet repudiated out of hand, we reach the end of Professor Cruickshank's chain of witness—each of whose reflections has served a minor but useful purpose in defining what a Simenon novel does not set out to achieve. And so on to M. Parinaud's cross-examination in chief.

M. Parinaud certainly plunges us 'into the middest'. He begins by noting that nearly all Simenon's adolescents, from the archetypal Roger of *Pedigree*, down through the young bomb-thrower Marette in the same novel, to 'Kiki' Donadieu and Michel Maudet of *L'Aîné des Ferchaux*, share a dominant characteristic. They are all in revolt, they wish to live violently against the grain of their surroundings—the monotony, mediocrity and misunderstanding that encompass them. In so far as Simenon's characters are concerned to follow out their destinies to the end of the chapter, how much do such decisions, accomplished in manhood, turn on these early dreams and strivings? For Simenon, the answer is quasi-physiological. In the case of most human-beings, he thinks, psychological growth, the capacity to absorb '*la matière*', ceases at about the age of eighteen. By that time the psyche has crystallised, the mould of character has been formed and hardened: everything gained after that age comes to human beings merely as experience, out of which something can be made—or, indeed, nothing, as happens in many cases. The time of absorption is over and for the rest of his life a man remains the determined slave of his childhood and adolescence. He, Simenon, is concerned with the kind of protagonist whose youth is already alive with aspirations and violent possibilities, possibilities that will later be realized and exteriorized in action. At this point he quotes Balzac: 'Without wishing to make any comparison with the Titan of the novel and myself.' Asked to give his idea of character in the novel, tell where and how he set about finding his heroes and how the fictional hero differed from the individual in real life, Balzac replied that while such a man could indeed be anybody (*'C'est n'importe qui dans la rue'*), he must be someone *'qui va jusqu'au bout de lui-même'*—in other words, someone who is journeying to the end of the night in terms of his own character. It is in this sense that all three—Balzac and Simenon actively as creators and M. Parinaud in his role of sympathetic critic—may be said to subscribe to Hegel's dictum that 'Destiny is man's consciousness of himself, but of himself as an enemy'.[1]

Each of us contains numerous possibilities within himself: seeds of the hero and the murderer, the saint, the mobster, the power-addict, the sexual maniac, the recluse. For a host of reasons —background, education, fear of the police, civilized *faiblesses* of all kinds—we only realize a small proportion of our fiercest drives and desires, taking care to stop short when these look like becoming dangerous to ourselves or society. In this way each real-life human-being kills a number of characters under him in the interests of ordinary living. The novelist's, or rather the story-teller's task, like that of the writer of tragedy, is to take a character—you, me, the man in the street—and push him to the end of himself, to give him the opportunity to enact the total 'paroxysm' of his personality. This can only be done by creating a situation in which the hero can play out his role to the full. Thus, having recognized the mood, the melodic line, the whiff of lilac, the inscape of the story—and this, as he (and, as we have seen, Romain Rolland) would insist, is an act of primary recognition rather than a strict part of the creative process—and, having placed the stage and the protagonist, it remains to set the trap, *le déclic*. This, Simenon tells Parinaud, is the only artificial element involved in the work in progress. Once again he emphasizes that there is no deliberate

[1] G. R. G. Mure: *The Philosophy of Hegel* (Oxford, 1966), pp. 47–48.

pre-plotting of the narrative. Does Simenon write to find a solution to certain human problems, asks Parinaud?—rather inconsequentially, one feels. The question merely gives Simenon a chance to parade his sceptical attitude to all human solutions while once again airing his therapeutic claim about needing to write as he needs to eat. No one, in view of his enormous output, would deny the truth of this assertion. Like the stage for Bernhardt, the writing of novels is indeed Simenon's rejuvenating battlefield; it does for him what glandular injections are supposed to do for other people. Yet at this point, and as if to rise to the height of the argument, I would prefer to substitute a passage from Nietzsche which would appear, albeit prophetically, to give a far better description of Simenon's creative dynamic than any explanation he has given us himself. It occurs in that section of *The Twilight of the Gods* headed 'Toward a psychology of the artist':

> If there is to be art, if there is to be any aesthetic doing and seeing, one physiological condition is indispensable: frenzy. Frenzy must first have enhanced the excitability of the whole machine; else there is no art. All kinds of frenzy, however diversely conditioned, have the strength to accomplish this: above all, the frenzy of sexual excitement, this most ancient and original form of frenzy.

Setting Parinaud's questionnaire aside for a moment, one should add that few writers' work is as saturated with sexual feeling as the fiction of Simenon. It is not only that so many of his plots turn on sexual conflict and the sexual act itself, or that sexual motifs—of betrayal, infatuation and so on—recur again and again in his novels. Nor is it only that the whole gamut of sexual emotion is revealed therein—from all the nuances of a bodiless and platonic love affair, wonderfully caught in the exchange of 'period' letters between Princesse de V——and the ex-ambassador in *Maigret et les Vieillards*, to the psychological ravages of impotence as described, for example, in that curious, highly ingenious and little-known masterpiece of melodrama, *Ceux de la Soif*. Rather, you might say that sex is the capsule in which most of Simenon's fiction is embedded. It encloses his novels, just as Time encloses Proust's *Recherche* or will and action enclose the world of Stendhal. In Simenon's case, Nietzsche's emphasis on the importance of 'this most ancient and original form of frenzy' is no mere generalization but has intense, specific reference to his whole creative nature and autonomy as an artist.[1] In fact sex bulks so largely, often so unconsciously, in his work as to suggest that it is the one separate creative bank account on which this most sparing and economical of writers has imaginatively overdrawn. Yet, if sexual feeling gives Simenon his driving force and his vision as a writer, one must agree that such withdrawals are compensated a thousandfold by the yield of the total investment.

Parinaud turns to the novel of the future, the fiction concerned with a new type of human being that our ever more complicated society is in the process of evolving. How far, in Narcejac's sense, is Simenon himself 'the novelist of a new beginning'? Foreswearing all claim to be a theorist of society, Simenon delivers a brief Voltairean fable. In the beginning, he says in effect, man began with a feeling of universal fear—fear of everything, fear of thunder, fear of the sea, fear of the dark. The last was his greatest terror. One imagines Adam and Eve whispering in the dark, during those white nights in Eden. 'Are you asleep?'—'No, and you?'—'But you're trembling?'—'Yes, I'm wondering if the sun will come back.' From this uncertainty, this cosmic fear, the first gods, sun, moon, wind, and so on, originated. Hardly had man reassured himself in this direction than he suffered a new phase of uncertainty—the fear of his fellow-men. Today we have reached a further phase. Man is afraid of himself. He goes in fear of the very means by which he hopes to realize his own destiny. As a result the pressures of guilt, fears of his unknown self lie heavier on man than at any period in his history. With guilt go its attendant-cousins, the feelings of inferiority and insecurity. Man feels himself inferior to his role in life: he watches his neighbour to see if he is faring better than himself. In other words, before he submits and becomes a robot man discusses his fate, in fear and trembling, with himself, not so much battling with his fellow-men, as passively comparing his fate with theirs. For Simenon's fear, in one form or another, lies at the root of almost all human evil.

[1] See the pertinent discussion on pp. 43–44 of Roger Stéphane's *Le Dossier Simenon* (Robert Laffont, 1961).

These sombre thoughts are succeeded by a train of scattered reflections, some of which have considerable bearing on Simenon's art and achievement. For example, there is his very typical contention that a man only lives his life out fully in his children and grandchildren and that he cannot be said to have completed his span as a human-being until the third generation. This fixated grandfather-father-son relationship, though it may have its real life source in *Pedigree*, is the theme of much of his fiction, most explicitly worked out, perhaps, in *L'Horloger d'Everton*. By one of Simenon's weird analogies, just as a man does not fulfil himself entirely in terms of his own life, so a novel cannot be judged to have been completed when its author writes 'The End', not even when it has been published. It takes at least two years for a book to come of age. The French-reading public, the critics and the wider, alien public who read the work in translation ('since I do not write for a single language') must all have read the book and been affected by it, before it can be said to have a life of its own.

This leads Simenon on to talk of the simple but highly individual style that he has invented for his kind of fiction. To the old *lycée* maxim that a writer should constantly seek to enlarge his vocabulary in the manner, say, of Giraudoux, Simenon suggests that on the contrary he should prune and reduce his vocabulary as much as possible; on the other hand, what strikes him most about the art of R. L. Stevenson is his manner of writing for a large public *'sans faire de concessions'*. Conrad, by making concessions of a different kind, could have reached a wider public and improved his style immensely at the same time, since many are put off by its calculated articulation. As for his contemporaries, their search for *le mot juste* is all very well but, after all, one writes to be read; if ninety per cent of your readers do not appreciate or even recognize the *mot juste* when they see it, what writer's end is served? By aiming at a universal vocabulary, a use of words that make the same sense in town or country, serve the same meaning in any kind of climate, region or community, Simenon, while aiming at the largest possible public, seeks to saturate his readers all the more in his own atmosphere and poetic vision.

Once more Simenon emphasizes the care he takes to exclude politics, religion, history and metaphysics from his work—

however much his readers, seeking between the lines, 'may divine my convictions, where they exist, or my tendencies'. He admits to his great interest in medical science and the part diagnosis plays in the shaping of his characters; he tells Parinaud how proud he was when an eminent specialist remarked that his men and women would not only exist at a romantic and intellectual level but in terms of their liver, lungs, heart, nerves and muscles. Asked to name his literary parentage, he chooses Gogol for his original tragi-comic attitude towards the world, as it is expressed in *Dead Souls*, and Tchekov, instancing the latter as the great artist of compassion (Simenon is presumably thinking less of the plays here than of Tchekov's short stories). In this connection he again cites Maigret and his role as a 'mender of destinies' (*raccommodeur des destinées*). As he again points out (and it is a fact that any consideration of Simenon's work must always take into account) he discovered the great Russians—Gogol, Dostoevsky, Pushkin (Tolstoy is unaccountably absent)—long before he read Balzac or Stendhal. Obviously, he much prefers the latter. And here, since we take leave of Parinaud at this point, a brief digression is once more in order.

As Simenon has explained many times, he finds Balzac materially stifling as a writer, while Balzac's primary aim—the construction of a vast, unified, inter-related society—is entirely alien to his own. Even where connections within Simenon's *tragédie humaine* might be supposed to exist, they are never explained. For example, is Donadieu, the ship's doctor and 'mender of destinies' of *45° à l'Ombre* any relation to the Donadieu shipping family of *Le Testament* or is Jaja of *Liberty Bar* the same as Gilles Mauvoisin's shady but good-hearted ally and counsellor in *Le Voyageur de la Toussaint*? Is Maigret's Dr. Pardon related to the Pardon of *Cécile est morte* or the Krull of *Chez Krull* to the Krull aboard the s.s. *Polarlys*, or M. Labbé the hatter to the policeman who hounds down the 'Man from Everywhere' in *Le Relais d'Alsace*? We are never told and certainly it never seems to matter —whereas Balzac, in whose work no human links are missing, would never allow such documentation to go by default.

Again, the driving force of Balzac's heroes is ambition—the ambition of a Rastignac, a de Marsay, a Maxime de Trailles 'to succeed! to succeed whatever the cost . . . We are as ravenous as wolves!'. Yet, just as none of Simenon's heroes are involved in the world's game, so even in their own lives they are protagonists in solitude: they lack the consolations of the daring throw made in common, they are without the clannishness of Balzac's power-seekers, they have none of what M. Félicien Marceau has termed 'the freemasonry of the Thirteen'. In their hates and duels and rivalries, Balzac's handsome creatures of prey are linked against the world; lone wolves, gathered from every obscure lair of the social steppe—bastardy, the provinces, the boulevard theatres, small-time journalism—they hunt as a genuine pack and form part of a common assault upon society. As though to give the lie to Sartre's castigatory remarks about Balzac's ignorance of his historical situation, M. Marceau comments on how a new predatory type emerges in the *Comédie* after 1830:

> Under the July Monarchy the lions or wolves gradually disappear
> . . . ambitious young men under Louis-Philippe choose other
> weapons. They become lawyers, like young Hulot, or Théodose de la
> Peyrade, or magistrates in the Court of Appeal. The day of elegance
> is over; a simple black suit creates a better effect. No more impertin-
> ence of manner either: it is the hearts of the electorate that these
> young men are out to win. And no more amorous intrigues:
> hypocrisy and a serious demeanour pay higher dividends.

For Balzac, obsessed by social flux, such variations of cast are the very stuff of the *Comédie humaine*; they are an essential part of the novelist's obligation to record his changing society. For Simenon, whose ideal aim, as he tells Parinaud, is to set each of his novels against a timeless contemporary background (or at least one that leaves them untied to any *époque déterminée*), the socio-historical scene, like everything else that touches the historical and the particular, is irrelevant. This leads us naturally on to consider the basic and impassable barrier that separates the solid, massively constructed, history-ridden and inter-connected world of Balzac, loaded with its properties and attributes, from the shifting, day-to-day mythological Ishmaelia created by Simenon. To do so is to realize the two fundamental paradoxes posed by Simenon's creativity: how can a writer be at once so fecund yet so uncomplicated? How can each of his characters and situations be so universal and at the same time so particular and concrete?

s.i.c.—6

The point has been discussed at length by Bernard de Fallois in his brilliant introductory essay.[1] As he says, a genius as prolific as Balzac may well write a hundred or more novels in an endeavour to construct a human comedy. Balzac, aiming at totality, saw his huge edifice in terms of a pyramid; Proust, aiming at unity, described the *Recherche* as a cathedral. Both were architects, both, in their vastly different ways, were didactic: their characters move and act according to certain psychological truths and along lines of human motive attested by their creators. But Simenon, just as he is no architect, no constructor or arranger of an *ensemble*, has no set patterns and no general truths to teach. He can only, so to speak, follow in the wake of his characters; he must search, with them, for the knowledge, gained in solitude, that they will teach him. Hence what de Fallois calls *'la modestie de ses personnages'*, who are not, strictly speaking, heroes in the usual sense—the sense, for example, in which we speak of Julien Sorel or Fabrizio as exemplars of Stendhal's principle of singularity. For Stendhal, who wrote for the Happy Few, the general mass of men and women are the foil, the lump, the scornable majority. Simenon's heroes belong to and are part of the general lump, they only emerge from it in the extremity of their destinies and situations. In Balzacian, Proustian and even Stendhalian terms, they are outside the realm of category and function. For Balzac a duchess is a duchess; what, he seems often to be asking himself, constitutes a duchess, what kind of a person can she be, just as Zola, in much the same way, asks himself what it is like to be a miner or a farmhand. But for Simenon the *clochard*, or M. Bouvet who would like to be a *clochard*, and the ex-Prime Minister are almost inter-changeable. For him they only begin to exist as individuals at the moment they go off the rails and take leave of their normal lives.

It is in this sense, as I said in Chapter 1, that Simenon is right to insist that the ex-Premier, though his attributes and general background are so like those of Clemenceau, owes nothing to the Tiger. Whereas (to go beyond M. de Fallois for a moment) as Balzac's critics pointed out many years ago, Eugène de Rastignac bore not only a striking likeness to the young Thiers in his

[1] *Simenon* (in the *Bibliothèque Idéale* series: Gallimard, 1961).

dandysme and his Southern origins (his blue cravats, 'the hint of garlic in his speech' and so on) but exhibited precisely those traits of character which are associated with Thiers, namely, lack of heart and aridity of feeling. As the critic Thibaudet (quoted by M. Marceau) put it: 'Everything is there, the Anzin mines as well as the love affair with his mother-in-law. Yet in 1830 the young and brilliant minister, Talleyrand's pupil and favourite, had nothing about him, either physically or morally, of the Prudhomme figure, at once so petty and so great, that M. Thiers was to become for his critics after 1871. It is as though Balzac, with the aid of his seven league boots, has anticipated history by forty years.' To anticipate history: this, indeed, is the magn-operative art of a Titan. It is the very opposite of the art of Simenon, public drama rather than private tragedy. To confront Simenon's ex-Premier with Balzac's Rastignac is to realize what M. de Fallois means when he says that while the novelist ordinarily interests himself in life, Simenon's fiction is nearly always primarily concerned with the death of the hero.

Chapter 5

AN IMPRESSION OF ISHMAELIA: PART I

MARCEAU divides his large-scale study of Balzac's world into two parts, Themes and Characters. Chapters on 'The Lions', old maids, young men, the worlds of literature and pleasure, etc., are followed by discussions of 'The Use of General Ideas', Love (and its 'Darker Aspects'), 'The Will to Power', 'The Theme of the Group', the quest for the Absolute, Time, Religion, Money, 'The Use of History', and so on. Most of these themes and categories are foreign to Simenon's fiction and I have not attempted anything like a systematic survey of his land of Ishmael after this manner. His world is certainly large enough but it is too unorganized. Paradoxically, it is also too contingent, too creatively homogeneous.

For all his bold fertility as a story teller, Simenon's novels spill over into one another in a manner peculiar to themselves. Sometimes it is the initial mood of a book that is bodily transferred— as happened, for example, when he temporarily laid aside *Le Train*, after writing the first twenty or so pages, because the development of the story seemed to conflict with the May-morning, First-Communion atmosphere that he wished to evoke and which he proceeded to carry over and express in *Maigret et les Vieillards*. More often it is a question of the same themes and situations either recurring with subtle variation or (and these are the true interior 'symmetries' of his fiction) repeating themselves but with different or even directly opposite results and consequences. As we have seen, Simenon displays an extraordinary, seemingly deliberate carelessness about such surface invention as the naming of his characters. Maudet, Maugin, Maugras, Maloin, Malou, Viau and Niau and Graux, Chave and Bauve and Bauche or the unspecified Krulls, Donadieus and Jajas—such cavalier labelling, almost numbering, must be done for a reason. Certainly, Simenon is not wilfully flouting the Balzacian canon of separate passport identity within the creative card-index system—a system as familiar to frequenters of the Rougon-Macquarts, the Guermantes, the Pallisers, the Forsytes, the Buddenbrooks or the Moskats as to those acquainted with the House of Nucingen. What reason, then, lies behind this calculated indifference to identity? Or is it, in fact, as deliberate as we suppose?

I think the answer is that it is a mixture of both. It is partly deliberate in the sense that in each of his novels Simenon seeks to blend the universal and the particular. Take Maloin, the Dieppois signalman of *L'Homme de Londres* (1934), for example. Quite by chance, from the elevation of his signal-box on the night-shift, Maloin witnesses a murder on the quayside. He becomes involved in the crime and, again quite by chance, ends by killing the murderer. Maloin could be anybody, he is part of that lump that the Stendhalian hero despises. Yet he is the protagonist of Simenon's novel and long before the novel ends the reader knows almost everything there is to know about him—and about his bothered and bothersome wife, his children, his small, noisy house on the cliffs, his dreadful in-laws, his secret and just conceit of himself as the *boule* champion of Dieppe and his exasperated determination not to reveal this fact to his wife unless she asks him. As a particular, concrete human-being, Maloin is quite unremarkable, an ordinary man making his way through life like the rest of us. And yet:

> It was absurd the way things had turned out, but such is life! And what rankled most was knowing they might so easily have turned out quite differently. Time and again it had hung on a thread . . .
>
> For instance, that night when Brown had started climbing the ladder leading to the signal-box and had stopped on the second rung. Supposing he'd come in, what would they have said to each other?
>
> And then that other time, when he'd followed Maloin all the way home without venturing to speak to him—when all the time Maloin had been prepared to hand over the suitcase . . .
>
> The last chance had been this very morning when he, Maloin, had brought the food to the boatshed. Supposing the man had answered him and they'd had a talk? What arrangement would the

two of them have come to? And with what consequences for the future of the two households on either side of the Channel, the two women, the four children?

Chance or 'the way things fall out'—it is this and no conventionally tragic role that gives Maloin his universal status. Things are bound to happen to a Macbeth or a Medea, their very 'diversity of state' argues the presence of tragedy. Whereas what happens to Maloin might happen to Malou, Maugras or, indeed, to any of us. He is the 'new type of man' in fiction, the particular human being caught up in the universal net of accident, whose image, startlingly presented, is among Simenon's great contributions to the contemporary novel. He is Maloin and he is everyone, or rather, paradoxically, he is everyone in essence and Maloin *in motu proprio*.

Obviously, Maloin is an extreme instance of the un-singular Simenonian hero drawn from the mass. Yet, as we shall see in Chapter 6, even his most singular and apparently Stendhalian characters tend to wilt and fade into the mass on examination. At a first glance, Michel Maudet and Philippe Dargens, those vicious young provincials, seem to bear a striking resemblance to Julien Sorel; like Julien, and even more like Balzac's pack of wolves, they are aggressive, ambitious, supremely egoistic, determined to make their way come hell or high water. Yet in the event their *singularity* is only skin deep. Infirm of purpose, they are as much the victims of accident (of fortunate accident, perhaps, in the case of Maudet) as poor Maloin himself. It is not what they *are*, in Sorel's sense, or even of how they *act*, in the sense of a Rastignac or a Lucien de Rubempré, as *what happens to them* that gives them their hold on our imagination. As always in Simenon's novels, the impulses of the drama comes from without. (In Maigret's wonderful and inexhaustible series, the case is, of course, just the opposite.)

Much of the fluid, shapeless, interchangeable nature of Simenon's characters is due to the fact that chance, accident, destiny, whatever you choose to call it, is so much stronger than the amount of free will in their lives. Looking back at Simenon's life, in comparison with that of the children of his imagination, one is almost tempted to imagine that, having crammed so much will and energy into his own achievement, he has little but the homogeneous cold comfort of predestination left to offer them. It is this, I think, more than his cinematic technique even, that accounts for the surprising lack of psychological change or development in his men and women. Virtually no one in a Simenon novel ever rises a sadder or wiser man through experience—or if he does so, as in the case of Ferdinand Grau or the youngest of the Malous, it is not so much through his own effort as because his creator has extended a reprieve and decreed a happy ending or at least one that augurs well for the future. The god's mood has changed; he has turned from a tragic to what, in Euripidean terms, might be called a 'quasi-satyric' solution. Creatively, there is something very Gaullist about Simenon. To a greater extent than any novelist in this century, he believes in holding all the threads in his own hand, and perhaps it is this, more than anything else about his work, that causes many readers to find his imaginary world as psychologically stifling as he himself finds Balzac's stifling and smothered in stage properties. He is as absolute and arbitrary as Zeus and—we are about to see—as unfathomable, under certain aspects, as Jehovah.

Interchangeable characterization, at least at surface level, unfathomable judgments—such adjectives require illustration. Without intruding on Maigret's preserves—since it is an early and a more or less straightforward case, certainly a very minor one—compare the outward trappings and characters of *Chez les Flamands* (1932) with *Chez Krull* (1939), one of the strangest and most ambiguous of Simenon's dramas. In both the basic setting is the same—a combined grocery-cum-chandler's store which serves drinks, run for a poverty-stricken bargee clientèle on the outskirts of a small French frontier town. The Peeterses are Flemish, the Krulls are of German origin; both families are long-settled prosperous aliens in a district rife with xenophobia. (This, incidentally, is a group-emotion that Simenon, perhaps because of his own mixed background, excels in describing. His novels explore every variety of it from polite distaste [*Les Fantômes du Chapelier*], through grudging, almost hostile indifference [*Le Petit Homme d'Arkhangelsk*] to the rabid manifestations of *Chez Krull* itself.) In both families there is a busy matriarch named Maria, an elder sister named Anna and an awkward, gangling, sexually-frustrated student and brother named Joseph. In each book the brother is attached to an identical fluffy, pink-and-white, moneyed fiancée named Marguerite and in each he is falsely accused of murdering a local slut. In both books the impulse comes from without: Maigret solves the Peeters murder while Hans, the Krulls' young German cousin, disrupts the family and abruptly decamps, leaving the Krulls to reassemble themselves with one piece missing. Hans's uncle, Cornelius, the old deaf paterfamilias and tranquil mystification of the family, hangs himself in his workroom, for no apparent reason except the monotony and general bloodiness of life chez Krull of which he, alone among them, had until then seemed totally unaware:

> He had hanged himself, they didn't quite know why. But did they know why he, the wanderer, had settled here on the outskirts of the town, why, for years on end, he had lived his life silently in this workshop, with the hunchbacked assistant?
> What did they know about him?
> He had arrived all alone. He had stayed there, alone in the midst of his family, with his patriarchal beard and his mysterious or serene face. He had gone away all alone, he had hanged himself in his corner, beside his chair with the sawn-off legs and a white wicker basket which would never be finished.
> He had said nothing, and it was a little terrifying, now, to wonder how much he had known.
> One was tempted to imagine that he had not merely come from Emden, like any journeyman touring Germany and France, but that he came from much further away in space and time, from a world fixed in Bible pictures, in church carvings and stained-glass windows.

So far as what Simenon chooses to tell us goes, Cornelius's life and death do seem inexplicable, as Biblically unfathomable as God's rejection of Esau's gifts or that extraordinary nocturnal moment, a moment that even Jung's talent for 'instant' exegesis was unable to interpret satisfactorily, in which He sought to kill His chosen servant Moses. As for Hans himself, he is one of the most ambiguous and interesting of Simenon's creatures—part Asmodaeus (and in this sense a vague presentiment of Frank in the first two sections of *La Neige était sale*) but much more, in his dreadful honesty of vision as in his deliberate malevolence and mischief, a projection of the mediaeval Vice. It is Hans who explains his poor-spirited cousin Joseph to himself and, in doing so, throws Joseph a life-line out of the Krull Slough of Despond:

> . . . Hans helped himself! He had even wanted to spend some time in a house like the Krulls', to sniff up its pleasant smells, to shock Anna, to frighten Aunt Maria, to drive Joseph to distraction and to make love with Liesbeth, teaching her the most indecent practices.
>
> He had wanted to, and he'd done it!
>
> And when, in due course, he would want to move on . . .
>
> 'You see, Joseph, in my opinion you'll always be unhappy . . .'
>
> 'Because I'm not like other people!' Joseph burst out. 'Because I'm a foreigner wherever I go! Because my feelings are different! Because I've no country, no countrymen, no people who think the way I do! Because I was born on a kind of island and my own family can't understand me . . .'
>
> 'I do it on purpose!' declared Hans.
>
> 'What?'
>
> 'Being different from other people! That's why they respect me . . . If I'd come politely asking you to put me up, admitting that I hadn't a penny and didn't know what to do . . . And if I'd told Liesbeth she was pretty and I was in love with her, instead of just toppling her backwards on her bed . . .'
>
> Joseph was closer than ever to shedding tears. His hands had trembled. He had blushed. Now he was at a loss. He wanted to beg Hans to go away at once, and was equally tempted to ask him to stay.
>
> He was afraid of him and needed him. Since they had been together in this room, since it had been proved that words could clear the air, banish terrors, reduce complex ideas to harmless simplicity, he had begun to dread solitude.
>
> He was not yet beaten, however. He was watching his cousin, trying to find arguments against him, striving to hate him in spite of everything.
>
> Both of them had forgotten the three women downstairs, and Cornelius in the workshop with the man.
>
> The room was almost a real student's room now . . .
>
> 'So here you are?' murmured Aunt Maria, looking from one to the other.
>
> She could scarcely hide her astonishment, perhaps her uneasiness. She must have found the atmosphere in her son's room unexpected.
>
> Hans was sitting sideways to the window, both feet on the sill. Joseph was leaning on the mantelpiece, next to the clock which always said ten to twelve.

And both faces were grave, with a gravity that had nothing tragic about it, the gravity of young men peacefully discussing eternal problems.

For Joseph, liberty, the freedom to be like other people, not 'to copy them clumsily, convinced you'll never make a good job of it' so that they themselves feel that you are both 'too much and not enough', will remain a mirage. As we realize in the epilogue to the novel, the chance that Hans suggests to him is a chance that Simenon will not allow him to take.

If Hans and Cornelius are the two unfathomable poles of *Chez Krull*, Hans is the dark angel, the catalyst who explodes the situation, exploits it and decamps, leaving havoc in his wake. In *Chez les Flamands*, the novel's *roman policier* prototype of seven years before, Maigret merely solves a mystery. Yet psychologically the link between the two books goes beyond the drawing-board similarities that we have noted. For example, Maigret's surprise at the way *his* dismal and ineffectual Joseph is worshipped by the Peeters womenfolk corresponds to Hans's astonishment as he realizes the nature of Maria Krull's scheme for diverting suspicion from *her* Joseph by arranging for Hans himself to disappear:

> Her breast heaving with optimism beneath its corset, she gazed at him with all her strength, as though trying to hypnotise him, to wrest agreement from him.
> 'You have nothing to lose! Once you're across the frontier . . .'
> So that was what she'd been aiming at! Hans, though not easily astonished, was completely bowled over this time. He admired his aunt, who had engineered all this conversation in order to explain to him:
> 'We could have you put in prison as a swindler. You have seduced Liesbeth. You have brought trouble and disturbance into the household, but none of that matters, provided you will agree to act the scapegoat and draw off suspicion from Joseph!'
> Joseph increased in stature because this woman had thought up such a plan for him. And meanwhile he was overhead, beside his open window, bending over his books!
> In the kitchen Anna and Liesbeth were waiting.
> 'I know these people and I'm sure they will leave us in peace . . .' she concluded in a toneless voice, turning to look out of the window.
> And the word 'people', which constantly recurred in her talk and in the family's coversation, had a special, almost threatening sound

in the mouth of a Krull. 'People' were all the rest of the human race, were a living ocean, surrounding the little island formed by the family. This ocean began at the Guérins' and stretched to the ends of the earth . . .

In its nature *Chez Krull* is a much more complex piece of fiction than Maigret's relatively simple adventure. It contains the seeds of another theme dear to Simenon, one akin to his 'symmetry' of opposed ends and consequences—namely, the identity of human opposites. When Hans realizes that the hidden and mysterious bond that unites his staid Aunt Maria and Pipi, the murdered girl's old soak of a mother, is 'a mixture of attraction and hatred, a need now and again to try each other's strength', he reflects that 'they are alike in the way Joseph and I are alike!'. Later, he tells Liesbeth 'I am like Joseph or rather Joseph's like me . . . Just as your mother might have been Pipi . . . What's more, I bet there are times when she envies her'; again, he tells himself that 'He could have been Joseph and himself simultaneously! He would have been able, all on his own, to play both parts, to take both sides of the conversation . . . Whereas Joseph was merely Joseph'. But here this two-way road of opposite identities forks abruptly. If Maria's envy of Pipi's totally carefree and degraded existence branches forward to M. Bouvet's dreams of living a *clochard*'s life with 'the Professor' on the Paris quaysides, Hans's recognition of himself as the protean player of parts leads us back in a roundabout fashion to the creative starting-point of Simenon himself.

Simenon's immense fecundity, plus his virtuoso ability to double back on his creative tracks in the manner described, makes it difficult—perhaps impossible and certainly rather useless—to attempt a strict chronological analysis of his work in the hope of making something like a consecutive or evolving pattern out of it. With two major exceptions—first, in the character of Maigret himself, secondly, in the creative 'break-through' of the last five or six years—his work presents no inner line of development strong enough to support a hypothesis of this kind. A look at the chronology of the work itself is, or should be, enough to deter the pattern-seekers. Take the years 1940 to 1950, for example. Seemingly, if we leave out everything he has written since *Le*

Train (1961), this period might be said to be the high watermark
of Simenon's fiction. Beginning with *Les Inconnus dans la Maison*
(1940), we have *Cour d'Assises* (finished in '37, but first published
in 1941 along with *Le Voyageur de la Toussaint*), *L'Aîné des
Ferchaux* (1945), *Lettre à mon Juge* and *Le Destin des Malou*
(both in 1947), *Pedigree* itself in 1948, followed by *Le Bilan
Malétras* and *La Neige était sale* in the same year, *Les Fantômes
du Chapelier* (1949), and *Les Volets Verts*, *L'Enterrement de
Monsieur Bouvet* and *Tante Jeanne*, all in 1950—a magnificent
roll-call, only a dozen out of thirty-six 'straight' titles, together
with thirteen Maigrets, among them the outstanding *Signé
Picpus*, the *Mémoires* and *Maigret à New York*. One might say
with justice that the heartland of Simenon's achievement lies in
this decade. The whole range of his moods and invention are on
view. From tragedy and genuine pathos (represented by Avaloine
in the *Lettre* and Maugin in *Les Volets* respectively), through
the Dostoevskyan horror of *La Neige* and the high obsessive
drama of Maudet and Ferchaux, by way of M. Bouvet's series of
fugues or flights from conventional reality and the romanesque
melodrama of the hatter (a book that plays the same startling part
in Simenon's work as *The Bells* played in Irving's acting), to the
heartening wisdom of *Tante Jeanne* and young Malou's resolve
to shoulder the burden of manhood—the total spectrum of
Simenon's art, if one includes the three Maigrets, is displayed in
these fifteen volumes, his whole palette of colours has been used
in their creation.

Yet to set this creative lustre apart from the rest of his achievement would be unnatural and tendentious. Though each of
Simenon's tragedies is unrelated and autonomous, a work of
fiction in its own right, his whole *tragédie humaine*, still happily
uncompleted, is one and indivisible: taken as a whole, it presents
such an ambiguous Janus face that it can only be looked at in
the round—that is to say, backwards and forwards at the same
time, with no concession to artificial divisions or contrived phases
and developments. At its best, beyond a certain intrinsic high
standard of its own, Simenon's fiction has no head or tail, no
before or after, no tidy sequence of imaginative rhyme and reason.
The sombre, sinister *haut bourgeois* world of La Rochelle that

uncoils itself under the bewildered eye of Gilles Mauvoisin in *Le Voyageur* is no projection of that earlier and, in some respects, more sombre and intimidating citadel of the provincial upper middle class, *Le Testament Donadieu*: the city, the *venue*, the atmosphere are the same; the theme, the intention, the design are entirely different. (The mere fact that the character of Gilles himself, the stranger returned, is the dominant and unifying force of the first book, while the Oresteian doom that dogs the whole Donadieu family is the real protagonist of *Le Testament* is in itself sufficient evidence of this.) Whatever the below-surface links between the two Krulls may be, there is certainly no inner line of development here. Similarly the death of Maugin, the great comedian of *Les Volets Verts*, cannot be said to look forward to the death of the ex-Prime Minister or sideways at the death of Bouvet.

Again, take Simenon in his reprieving mood. In a superficial sense you could say that the heroism of Tante Jeanne or of Alain Malou have long been anticipated, that Ferdinand Graux, the Congo planter of *Le Blanc à Lunettes* (1937) and Chave, the Belgian anarchist-hero of *Le Suspect* (1938), have been before them in gaining their creator's goodwill. All four have surmounted their illusions, their infatuations, or, in Malou's case particularly, their disgusts. Like Don Quixote, they can all say, sadly or proudly after their fashion, 'I was mad once, but I am sane now.' All four have made a return to reality, to real duties, to the world of the living and yet, because the context of reality has been different in each case, for each of them the new path towards reality is individual and separate. Grau, somehow saved by Referee Simenon's bell, is cured of his besotted passion for the strange Englishwoman who has torn his life up by the roots and suffered to return to his fiancée Emmeline (brave, quiet, loyal, intelligent and good, with beauty thrown in, the perfect bourgeois heroine of Molière's imagination!) and to his humdrum life as a coffee planter; Chave, spent by his efforts to save his accomplice Robert and tired of his puppet-stage struggle to right the world's wrongs and change society, goes back to his wife and child and his job as a theatrical prompter and handyman (the irony of occupation?); as for Tante Jeanne, having played *dea ex machina* to her brother's worthless family, following the discovery of his suicide, she disappears into her cloudscape of vagabond fecklessness, secure in the knowledge that she can save others, even if she cannot save herself; Malou, with the grimmest and heaviest inheritance of them all, is left with the best chance of all—the time to remake his life. Each of them responds bravely, or fortunately, to his or her situation—and, in doing so, acts in favourable contrast to the majority of Simenon's unfortunates. Yet, even so, each only witnesses once more to the single negative generalization that it is possible to make about Simenon's field of folk—namely, that in all their tragedies or near escapes from tragedy, their fugues or their returns, the reader, if he is honest, can discern no pattern of any kind, no message, no great general truth, no psychological progression or line of moral development, but only a succession of unceasing variations on the theme of particular destiny and universal accident.

Perhaps something of this despairing realization accounts for the actual way in which many people do read Simenon—that is to say, compulsively, rather in the manner that Martin Turnell's Frenchman admitted to his reading Balzac and as Gide in his *Journals* admits to reading Simenon's novels. His tragedies travel so quickly, so cinematically, across the path of our imagination as to leave us sometimes expectant, out of breath, even a shade resentful, feeling, as Miss Brophy might say, cheated out of a full ending, of a real catharsis. Yet the fact that these checks and disappointments can occur anywhere in Simenon's work, spoiling our enjoyment of the lateish and otherwise exciting *Les Complices* (1955) as much as the early and near-perfect *Faubourg* (1937), proves how impossible it is to apply system and chronology to such prodigious creation. Better, perhaps, if we view Simenon's Ishmaelia impressionistically, making our way without critical maps and handbooks. The question then arises, at which point in that long coastline should we enter the interior?

I propose to do so at Matadi, a port in French Equatorial Africa, by way of *45° à l'Ombre* (1936), embarking on the ss. *Aquitaine*, homeward bound for Bordeaux. From his first 'straight'

novel (*Le Passager du 'Polarlys'*, 1932) onwards, all Simenon's
ships are unhappy ones, but the *Aquitaine* is unhappier than most.
Even while she is still in port, before the return voyage has begun,
the ship appears to be making water; also, some displacement in
the ballast is causing it to list. No real danger, the Chief Engineer
assures Donadieu, the ship's doctor, but the pumps must be
worked discreetly so as not to alarm the passengers, some of whom
have already been questioning the stewards . . .

And what a passenger-list! Lachaux, an old *crapule*, the richest
trader in the colony, rumoured to sweat his white employees as
hard as he beats his niggers, an arch-grumbler and trouble-maker,
well-known on this line, a man whose mere presence on board
is enough to cast an evil eye on any ship. There are the Bassots:
he, an Army medical officer, suspected of insanity, is being
invalided home—vaguely under surveillance, he takes his meals
in his cabin but displays a disquieting restiveness on deck; his
wife (heartless? a bitch? tired of it all?) is already getting high on
champagne and dancing old-fashioned tangoes with the three
military bachelors, uninhibitedly going on leave. There is M.
Dassonville (ex-polytechnician '*avec un bon numéro*', first-class,
Captain's table) absorbed in his figures, getting off the ship two
stops ahead anyway, thus leaving his elegant, homeward-bound
wife to the predatory advances of M. de Neuville, the ship's
police official, public entertainments officer and professional
ladies' man—the only human-being who seems to be enjoying
the trip. Lastly, there are the Hurets, a young couple, forced
home by the climate. They are also travelling first-class by
courtesy of the shipping line because they have a sick baby.
Huret himself, a junior clerk in a firm at Brazzaville, is obviously
without means.

At the next port of call, to complete this sombre picture, the
ship is due to take on three hundred Annamite troops who are
being shipped back to their own country after doing a long spell
of coolie-labour constructing railways in the interior. By page 40
the first of them has been quietly buried at sea in the early hours
of the morning and Donadieu in his turn is playing down the
Chief Engineer's suspicions of yellow fever. The burial itself,
with the flawlessly turned out Mme. Dassonville watching from

the Captain's bridge, an interested, embarrassing spectator, is wonderfully described, as good a brief, impersonal moment as Simenon has ever captured. In the space of six pages he manages to convey a sense of everything that Gide (in *Voyage au Congo*) or Malraux (in *La Tentation de l'Occident*) condemn about the colonial heart of darkness, without moving a muscle. Simenon may not have much in common with Flaubert, but in his determination not to pass judgment but rather to let the horror speak for itself, he is certainly the Master's equal.

Slowly the ship makes its way up the coast of West Africa—Port Bouet, Libreville, Dakar. Passengers disembark, new ones come aboard; the Chief Engineer works away at his pumping; Donadieu, lying in his cabin, reads Conrad and smokes his carefully-measured quantities of opium. The *Aquitaine*'s original knot of passengers continue pacing the deck of their individual destinies. Distractions are organized, a sweepstake, a noisy, drunken fancy-dress party; quarrels break out, sun-helmets are discarded, warmer clothing donned. All the while tension mounts. The second Annamite dies; Captain Bassot, after finally running amok, is put under restraint—but how mad is he, thinks Donadieu, catching Bassot's ambiguous and expressive wink as he turns the key of the ship's cell? (It is a question that many of Simenon's characters are to ask of one another in the years and the books that follow.) Huret, whose child is now certainly dying, has likewise gone berserk. He is taking heavily to the bottle, gambling feverishly and generally unsuccessfully, borrowing money to pay his I.O.U.s and his bar chits. Then, suddenly, he is accused of stealing a wallet.

What on earth, thinks the reader, now completely obsessed by the *Aquitaine*'s voyage home and all these banal, unfortunate or plainly appalling human-beings aboard her, what on earth is the upshot of all this going to be? How will the *dénouement* occur? Through man's agency or a plain Act of God in the Atlantic? After all, the reader goes on to reflect, now suspecting a sell-out, there are not many pages to go . . .

And a sell-out it is. Suddenly we are in sight of Bordeaux, the seagulls are screaming overhead, the cabin luggage is packed, the purser has squared his accounts, everything has been adjusted, the voyage is over. The Hurets' baby has been saved, and Huret himself, having luckily almost broken his leg, has been spared further complications on board ship and left to fight his poor young man's battle with fate and his family once more on *terra firma*. Lachaux disappears down the gangplank 'like an Eastern potentate', the truth about his lost wallet for ever a mystery. Mme. Dassonville slips discreetly away, Dr. Bassot is placed in the ambulance (his wife now in a black dress with her face composed to match). The *Aquitaine* goes into dry dock for repairs. Only Donadieu is left, thinking about his patients, and about how, once more on this voyage, he has been tempted into playing God-the-Father and how, on his next ship, he knows that he will do so again.

Although *45° à l'Ombre* has its compelling moments—it is, indeed, like most of Simenon, compulsively readable—it is not an entirely successful novel. Wrongly, perhaps, yet understandably, the reader feels once more that he has been cheated of a proper ending. There has been no climax, no note of finality, certainly no catharsis—how could there be? The book ends, as all such voyages end, with goodbyes being waved and luggage loaded on taxis. Yet, in its impersonal, inconclusive fashion, it makes a good starting-point for an exploration of Ishmaelia. At the risk of appearing pompous, one might say that in embryo this book contains all the ingredients of the Simenonian universe. In its own highly-localized cabin-and-boat deck terms, it provides a scale-model of the background to the tragedies to come. The fact that the novel lacks a true protagonist of its own means that the stage is set and lit up for our inspection all the more clearly.

At first, it had seemed that Huret *was* a true protagonist, a man marked out for tragic destiny. Donadieu, the earliest of Simenon's menders of destinies, realizes this as soon as Huret comes aboard:

> He did not know why he felt more concerned about this young man than about his other passengers. Rather, he preferred not to admit to the reason.
> It was simply an intuition that he had when he first met anyone. Not a doctor's intuition. He had had it long before he chose his profession.
> As a schoolboy, when the winter term began, casting his eyes

around the newcomers, he would spot a face and tell himself: 'That one's marked down!' . . .

It was absurd. Donadieu had no gift of second sight. And his choice, so to speak, didn't necessarily fall on the boy who looked really ill . . .

It was subtler than that. To speak of it would have disturbed him, for he only half believed in the trick himself. He just sensed that certain human-beings are born to catastrophe as others to live out a long, peaceful life.

From the first moment he saw him, before he knew who Huret was or that he had a sick child, Huret's face has struck him in this way . . .

In fact, despite Donadieu's intuition, Huret's creator lets him off the hook—almost contemptuously, so it seems to the reader, tossing this very ordinary young man back into the common pool of humanity as a creature unworthy of real misfortune. He is reprieved, at least, for the time being.

Setting aside the necessarily inconclusive terms of the novel itself—the fact that it tells the story of a steamer's voyage home with the characters' lives ending on the dockside—the reader must still ask himself: in what way is Huret unworthy? Morally? Psychologically? Intellectually? Generally, in terms of his character? Or simply, because he is in fact a very ordinary, unstable young man trapped by poverty and responsibilities? Here, I think, one stumbles unexpectedly into the heart of Simenonian tragedy and of what I have termed, for the convenient purposes of this book, his type of tragic hero.

Agreed, that the sullen, shadowy, purposeless, drifting Huret is quite unremarkable. In class terms, he is a petty bourgeois without ambition (that is to say, in this respect he is unlike those other petty bourgeois, Philippe Dargens, De Ritter, Michel Maudet, Marcel Bauve, Steve Adams and the rest). That in itself, by the terms laid down throughout Simenon's fiction, should be no barrier to Huret's seeking entrance, as it were, to his creator's tragic club. Is he less remarkable than Petit-Louis (*Cours d'Assises*) or Elie Nagéar (*Le Locataire*) or Jean Passant-Monnayeur (*La Veuve Couderc*) or, for that matter, the Montmartre widower or the Little Man from Archangel?

True, like a crowd of other Simenon young men, Huret likes

to cut a dash, to assume an air—to flirt and, even more, to be seen flirting, with Mme. Dassonville, to stand everyone rounds of drinks in the ship's saloon, to be, however fleetingly, the centre of attention. In his case this is a means of forgetting the horrors of his life—his dying child in the cabin below, his wife's agony and outraged hatred, his knowledge that he is penniless and that disaster and probably prison await him at the end of the voyage. All this is what Donadieu sees in Huret's face at a first glance and why, as a diagnostician of misfortune, Donadieu finds Huret the most interesting, perhaps one should say the most *real*, person aboard ship.

Nor should this aspect of Donadieu's character be ignored. Just as Graham Greene's whisky-priest runs to embrace the sinner, so Donadieu, the opium-doctor, hugs misfortune like a lover (religion, in Simenon's terms, is appropriately relegated to the pair of White Fathers sleeping peacefully in their second-class deck-chairs throughout the voyage). Having recognized Huret as the beloved victim, one of Fate's black chosen, Donadieu, in his psychologically contradictory capacity of a life-healer or *mender* of destinies, does his best to call the young man back to the realities of his situation. He lends Huret money and saves his child, while life itself, by causing Huret to fall over a ship's cable and thus be spared any further immediate complications, does the rest. At which point Donadieu, and certainly Simenon, cease to take any further interest in him.

For a moment Huret has been touched by the god. But he has not been chosen. Having taken a second look at him, Fate has shruggingly tossed Huret aside. In the factory of tragic destinies he is, fortunately for himself, one of her rejects, a flawed vessel, an imperfect transmitter of Atropos. Not for any defect in Huret himself—that, as we have seen, would be no hindrance—nor, to put it simply and crudely, because his creator can no longer be bothered with him. On the face of it this would seem to be the most probable explanation; certainly it is the one most likely to be advanced by those who regard Simenon as a fundamentally un-serious writer.

Personally, I cannot accept this explanation—chiefly because Simenon's work contains so many instances of destiny not accompanying a man or woman all the way to the tragic end envisaged. Again and again, in the case of Chave, of Maudet, of Graux, of Gobillot, of Jonsac, Joseph Timar, Emile and countless others, Fate, for various reasons, refuses to go the whole hog. That she refuses to do so in the case of Huret is owing, I think— if an expounder of Simenon's universe may quote Scripture for the purposes of his argument—simply to the fact that the ways of Providence are inscrutable. As he contemplates Huret in mid-voyage, Donadieu remembers his confessor at school telling him that, although man was free of his acts, from the beginning of the world God knew everything that was to befall each human being. Accordingly, waiting for the 'almost mathematical' moment when disaster will strike the young man, the doctor finds himself almost wishing for it to happen, growing impatient when it does not arrive. And yet, *viae Dei impenetrabiles sunt*. Mulling it all over in retrospect, as he leans across the ship's rails and watches the *Aquitaine*'s passengers take their leave, that would seem to be Donadieu's text. Or, in other words, the spirit of tragedy blows where it lists.

In the case of Marcel Viau, the hero of *Au Bout du Rouleau* (1947), the tragic spirit may be said to blow directly, heavily, consistently and to predestined purpose. This novel does not rank high in the Simenon canon, yet to my mind it is one of the most mysterious and disquieting of all his books. In terms of strict progression towards inevitable catastrophe, it is the purest of his minor works of fiction.

Technically, the book might be described as a Novel of Pursuit,[1] for Viau, a small-time amateur in his early thirties, is on the run for a robbery-with-violence committed outside a nightspot in Montpellier, having recently bungled a con job elsewhere. A peasant from Anjou by origin, he has passed himself off as the son of a prosperous Swiss businessman who has been sent into

[1] See the outline of George Granger's lecture 'From Godwin to Graham Greene' in Roy Fuller's superb thriller, *The Second Curtain* (1953), itself a classic of disquiet and mystery.

the Midi to learn wine-growing. Installed as an unpaid apprentice in the household of a rich local grower, he has succeeded in courting the daughter of the house and has tacitly been accepted as her fiancé by the family. His real identity having been discovered, he has been threatened with the police and forced to pack his traps. Hence the assault upon the fuddled victim with the briefcase outside the *boîte*. Here again, Viau has been unlucky. He has not hit hard enough. The man has recovered and given the police the numbers of the missing banknotes. Viau, now at Toulouse where he has picked up a dance-hostess named Sylvie, has had to flush his gains down a brasserie toilet and take to flight again, accompanied by the girl. Now, after six days on the run, they have reached Chantournais, a small market town near La Rochelle, in the neighbourhood of his father's farm.

The relationship between Viau and Sylvie is a curious one:

> He did not kiss her before going out. They never kissed. There seemed no question of love between them. What had happened was what happens with certain stray dogs; a dog you have never seen follows you in the street and, before you know it, has adopted you, never leaves you and takes you for its natural master . . .

Certainly, Sylvie—undemanding, unclinging, unreproachful, quietly dressed and spoken—is the ideal moll for a moody, discontented, secretive and desperate fellow like Viau. She never enquires what his plans are, never takes his arm in the street. Even the timidly casual manner in which she asks him if he doesn't think he is drinking too much, is said in a way that shows she is 'a woman who knows how to speak to men, at any rate to men like Viau'. Down to their last few hundred francs, the couple have installed themselves in a seedy, depressing hotel presided over by M. Maurice, a mysterious old gentleman, soft-spoken, drolly *ci-devant*, distinguished in a faintly raffish but deprecating way. He reminds Viau of a certain kind of stewed elderly Englishman he has met in bars.

As the action develops, it becomes clear that Viau is something more than an ordinary, small-time crook. By definition he is certainly a 'member of the criminal classes' but his code is so complicated yet so impassioned that, psychologically speaking, he can scarcely be described as a criminal. Viau's actions, however disgraceful, arise out of a state of rage and resentment—a self-justified, inarticulate and outwardly-directed resentment against things as they are and against the *larves* who manipulate 'the set-up' and draw their substance from it. Viau's anti-social feeling is partly intense and personal, derived from his rough life in the French colonial army and the Merchant Service, partly atavistic, the peasant's feeling of powerless rage in the face of all the middlemen in law, business and merchandise who seek to trick him on market day or tie him up in legal documents. Viau's particular character and crimes aside, this feeling breaks out like a rash all through Simenon's human repertory, forming yet one more contrast between his and Balzac's attitude to society. In the Human Comedy, as has been observed, peasants, as characters in their own right, are rare. It is the notaries, the buyers-up of bills, the foreclosers of mortgages, who are the subject of creative attention; the peasantry are so many passive and static objects to be fleeced and cheated. In Simenon's fiction, on the contrary, the emphasis is all the other way: it is those on the receiving end of the world's game, those who get slapped, who obtain full attention. The tricksters and middlemen are only there to precipitate the action. (They are, indeed, represented, in curiously old-fashioned and Balzacian terms, by Palud, the hole-and-corner pseudo-notary in *Dimanche* [1939].[1])

Like so many of his type, Viau is the dupe of his disgusts. His contempt and loathing of the *larves* leads him, on his first evening reconnoitre of the town, to get drunk in the eminently bourgeois and *larve*-ridden Café des Tilleuls where he is plucked like a pigeon at a card game. He leaves, owing Mangre, a middle-aged bankrupt wine merchant and the prize bad lot of the district,

---

[1] 'The name was familiar to him [Emile], as it used to be mentioned by his parents, who had had recourse on several occasions to this lawyer. For so he was called, although his profession was an ill-defined one. Not far from the Three Bells at Luçon he kept a grocery store with green-tinted windows where country people used to queue on market days.

'Palud had worked a number of years as a notary's clerk, then had started a business of his own, advising clients about their transactions, whether buying or selling goods, about wills, investments, or inheritances. In a semi-official capacity he also took care of their lawsuits, and he stood roughly in the same relation to real lawyers, real solicitors, or notaries, as a bone-setter or healer does to doctors.'

a large sum of money. It is obvious that no one, Mangre least
of all, believes that this card debt will be paid. Choked with
rancour and frustration, knowing that he is trapped in the town,
furious with Sylvie, who appears to have established some kind
of mysterious understanding with M. Maurice, Viau looks round
for a likely crib. He is resolved to pay Mangre his money next day
—not for honour's sake but because he and all the onlookers
in the café have politely disbelieved and quietly mocked him.
For Viau, the tearing up of his I.O.U. will be an act of
vengeance.

Instead of breaking and entering—which would give Viau the
kind of violent and 'equal' chance that his *jalousie de mâle*
demands—Sylvie persuades him to steal M. Maurice's savings
while the old man is temporarily absent, performing his nightly
act of sexual service to the hotel's elderly and unappetizing
proprietress. All against the grain, Viau steals the notes hidden
so predictably (how has Sylvie come to know of this?) in M.
Maurice's bedroom, behind a reproduction of Millet's *L'Angélus*.
The following day he repays Mangre, to everyone's astonishment
and, in a further card game, succeeds in cleaning out the wine
merchant. At once the mood of the café changes—or, rather, the
general *Schadenfreude* changes direction; his fellow-*larves* are
delighted that their local black sheep—who still enjoys a thread-
bare prestige through his connections and cannot be openly
snubbed—should have been skinned by the stranger. Later, Viau
learns that tax officials have arrived in the town and that Mangre
looks like being completely destroyed and probably arrested.
Impulsively, in one of those rainstorms that are such an atmospheric feature of Simenon's provincial life (M. Maurice with his
strange, mysterious affability, has insisted on lending him his
umbrella), Viau makes his way across the town to warn Mangre,
for whom he now feels only pity and a certain sympathy. But
Mangre, with his bed-ridden wife, his unenviable reputation and
his sea of criminally financial troubles, is anything but grateful.
Instead, he has a sardonic word of warning for Viau.

> 'Perhaps I am a *crapule*, but I am an intelligent one, a *crapule*
> with a freehold house and four farms, all well out of their clutches . . .
> Besides, I'm local, I've a pedigree, I play cards with the nobs . . . If

I've cheated, I've been careful to keep in with people who'll move heaven and earth to avoid scandal . . .

'Whereas you, thirty years old, you and your pretty mistress, you're no more than a shit bird of passage, an apprentice-*crapule*, with nothing behind you, no background and no front . . .

'Sooner or later, they'll realize that . . .

''That day it won't be me but you they'll be after . . .'

This last thought seemed to console him . . . he seemed to want Viau to feel frightened, was waiting for him to give way, was impatient at seeing him stay calm, was even a shade embarrassed . . .

The day is not long in coming. Laboriously but inevitably, the police are on Viau's trail. In vain Sylvie and M. Maurice, whose identity and previous relations with the girl have now been disclosed, implore Viau to save himself, making use of the means they have provided. He refuses, defies the police, barricades himself in his bedroom, is overpowered and taken. Later, he sharpens a soup spoon on the cemented floor of his cell and uses it to mortal effect as a razor.

Perhaps, his creator comments, Viau has at last found a true place for himself. Perhaps, as a punishment, he has been condemned to an eternal search for it.

> At any rate, as far as this world is concerned, he was dead. No one but Sylvie and M. Maurice, with a man whom neither of them knew but whom they realized was his father, was there at Viau's burial.
>
> Except for a figure in silhouette, standing a good way off on the pavement, who looked like M. Mangre.

Paraphrased baldly in this fashion, it is difficult to convey the precise nature of the strange, powerful impression that *Au Bout du Rouleau* makes upon the reader. This is largely because we are made to feel Viau far more intensely than we are concerned, or invited, to understand him. The ground-force of the book resides in its mystery—not the immediate mystery of the plot or the protagonist's response to his predicament, but the inarticulate, unformulated mystery of Viau himself and, even more, the hiddenness of other people's lives in relation to ourselves as represented by him. Each of the four human beings following his corpse has an interest, an emotional stake, in Viau, yet, in addition, their creator invests each with a mysterious personality of his or her own, only vaguely and partially disclosed through the role each of them has played in his tragedy. Here, once again, by a skilful use of false human perspective, Simenon adds a psychological twist to the narrative.

For example, take old Viau, the peasant father. He never accuses or reproaches his son, never questions him about his actions, receives him in the usual way without comment—and not at all as a prodigal son—when he chances to turn up. Nevertheless he represents the norm of Marcel's life, the standard from which Viau knows himself to have fallen and by which, in his camouflaged self-disgust, he affects to judge the world—but, ultimately, judges himself. Asleep, Viau dreams of his father; awake, though the old man's farm is close at hand and time is running out, he talks continually of taking Sylvie, also of peasant birth, to visit his father, yet avoids doing so until the chance is gone. Viau *père* is the lifeline that the son, in his moments of tragic and solitary self-awareness, realizes that he has long ago cut behind him. Yet what do we know of Viau's father, what circumstances in his life have determined his acceptance of things as they are?

Just as Marcel, by his previous acts, has severed himself from his father and his past, so Sylvie's devotion and M. Maurice's sad, conspiratorial good-will cannot persuade him to accept a lifeline for the future. All that either of them can do is to assuage Viau's here-and-now craving for status and consideration—his need to find 'a true place for himself' in his own and others' esteem. Viau's need to dominate, to be admired as a tough, cynical manipulator of life, is the consequence of knowing inside himself that he is an amateur, a small-timer, a *moindre* unable to forego his impulses, a passive not an active criminal, a bird of passage and chance misfortune. His forceful pseudo-*démarches*, his affected curtness, his half-drunken displays of callous brutality towards Sylvie, his absurd and pathetic need, in everything he does, to overplay his hand, is all part of an attempt to disguise his weakness from the world and from himself. Mangre, as we have seen, is there to remind Viau of his real situation—and later, by his hovering attendance at Viau's funeral, to cause the reader to ponder the hidden nature of Mangre's own tragedy.

Viau will sit up all night with M. Maurice in fictional re-
miniscence over a bottle of cognac, recounting his voyages in the
Merchant Navy, persuading himself that he was a ship's officer
and not a deckhand acting as steward. Yet he will not allow M.
Maurice (again, what is the real story behind *his* failure in life?)
or Sylvie, whose devotion, outwardly so dog-like, inwardly so
intelligent, Viau flaunts and squanders, to help him to freedom.
As for Sylvie herself, one can only say that if she is too young
to have much of a past, she lives in the reader's mind as one of
Simenon's most distinctive and appealing heroines.

Thus we are left with the genuine tragic hero himself. Viau's
manhood has been spent in the attempt to assert his solidarity
with other human-beings, to persuade himself that he belongs.
By taking his life he recognizes and affirms his solitude—his
realization, after all his boasting and make-believe, that he is not
only powerless against his individual destiny but that, because he
belongs to nothing and to nobody else, his 'true place' can only
be the one that Fate provides for him. Each of the four mourners
who follow his coffin—his mistress, his father, his enemy and his
friend—are unconsciously witnessing to their awareness of Viau
as a man tragically marked out and separate from themselves.
Only Mangre, it would seem, is aware of the mysterious corollary
that follows from this. It is one that runs through all Simenon's
genuine tragedies—namely, that if solitude or apartness is the
ultimate badge of human suffering, this supreme infliction may
be held to constitute, after its own terrible and paradoxical yet
lucid and inevitable law, a state of innocence. In Simenon's
inverted, 'human all-too-human' theology, solitariness (as it
were, privation) is the sign of the Elect.

Not all Simenon's heroes can boast a shadow as long as Viau's.
Vladimir, for example, the protagonist of *Chemin sans Issue*
(1938), only grows his shadow in the last chapter of the book.
This sombre tale of betrayal and expiation begins on a deceptive
note of frivolity and staleness amid the dregs of cosmopolitan
café society in an establishment on the Riviera. Only after
Vladimir has betrayed his comrade, Blinis, and murdered his

mistress Jeanne, one of Simenon's prize spoiled millionairesses ready-made for the chopper, does the novel suddenly find itself, having moved a Dostoevskian world away to the night shelter in Warsaw where Vladimir vainly searches for the friend he has wronged:

At last the Shelter loomed up through the shadows: an enormous building with the aspect of a medieval prison. Dim forms were prowling round it, and at first Vladimir wondered why they did not enter. Then, as he went up the steps, a voice hailed him from a recess beside the door.

He was being asked for a trifling sum, the smallest Polish coin. Which explained why that ragged crew remained outside; none had even a copper in his pocket. They were hanging about on the off-chance that there might be some free berths at closing-time.

Inside, the air was foul and stagnant: at every step one stumbled over bodies stretched or curled up on the floor, even in the passages. To right and left were big barn-like rooms the walls of which were lined with bunks, as on a ship, but here were tiers and tiers of them right up to the ceiling, and each bunk contained a man, sometimes two or three. Others were squatting on the floor, or leaning against stanchions. Some had partly undressed and were bare to the waist. The majority were elderly, and there was a sprinkling of patriarchal greybeards, but one saw young men too, with gaunt, famished faces . . .

Vladimir was beginning to lose hope. There must be fully a thousand men here, perhaps more; for, apparently, there were more rooms of the same kind on a higher floor, to which a staircase gave access. What chance had he of finding Blinis in this human ant-hill? Probably the best course would be to go from room to room calling his name: only he didn't dare . . .

Suddenly there was a metallic buzz, so like the sound of a telephone-bell that, for a moment, Vladimir was taken in, and half imagined all this had been a dream from which a telephone-call was rousing him. The men in the bunks sat up, grumbling, while those lying on the floor rose slowly to their feet, blinking their eyes.

A priest came in, a man in his thirties, wearing a full beard. As he walked slowly down the central passage, the men made way for him, gazing at him lethargically, without affection as without hostility. He opened a black book he was carrying, cleared his throat, and cast a tranquil glance around before crossing himself with sweeping movements that the others copied, more or less decorously.

Meanwhile a feeling was growing in Vladimir that his presence here was resented; at any moment all these down-and-outs might make a rush at him and hustle him out, if not worse . . .

The brief service was ended. Everyone began talking, or went back to bed. No more notice was taken of the priest, who walked out with the same slow, tranquil step as he had entered.

And then, suddenly, Vladimir's eyes filled with tears, something seemed to snap inside him, and he heard himself crying brokenly: 'Blinis! Blinis!'

Contentedly—too contentedly, the reader may feel, for a Simenon hero first-class, though, of course, in this case the hero is a Slav—Vladimir sets his friend on his way back to happiness in France and takes his place as a rower in the galleys of misfortune:

For, in his drunken mood, an idea had germinated; he must make expiation. It was up to him to live through every one of Blinis's experiences, stage by stage, and wind up, bearded and derelict, with no shirt under his coat, in the Night Shelter . . .

. . . It pleased him to know that, by agreeably slow degrees, he was going the same road as Blinis; the road that ended at the Shelter. So everything was for the best. The more he thought things over, the more convinced he was of this.

Its other qualities apart, *Chemin sans Issue* is notable for the fact that although Simenon's fiction abounds in cases of passive remorse, his characters seldom exhibit active repentance of this kind. Intelligent and disinterested goodness is not rare among them—here once more Simenon differs from Balzac whose moral world can be divided, with rough but sufficient justice, into rogues and fools. (This is, in fact, one of the main objections to the psychology of the *Comédie Humaine*.) But total reparation of the kind displayed by Vladimir is infrequent enough in real life to merit more than this single and singular mention in Simenon's spectrum of human motive.

If Vladimir's shadow is shorter than Viau's, some of Simenon's most actively memorable heroes may be said to cast little or no shadow at all. Such a one is Petit-Louis, the protagonist of *Cour d'Assises* (1941). This grimly effective piece of story-telling is a good example of Simenon's giving Sim his head not only in the construction but also in the characterization of a novel, with surprisingly successful results. (*L'Evadé* [1936], the tale of an escaped convict who poses successfully for some twenty years as a model schoolmaster, and *Le Rapport du Gendarme* [1944], a puzzle of peasant identities, are good examples of Sim at his creative second-best.) The whole atmosphere of the book—set mainly in Nice and on the Isle of Porquerolles—is in complete contrast to the opaque, umbrageous setting of Viau's duel with Fate. A hard, white Mediterranean light beats down on Petit-Louis's criminal doings and those of his associates. One has only to compare the two books to see that Simenon's insistence, in his talks with Parinaud, on the importance of determining the mood or 'melodic line' of a novel before settling anything else, is not mere creator's sales-talk but a genuine explanation of his method of approach.

A miner's son from the North, dragged up as an evacuee in the First World War by his sluttish, hyper-odious mother, Petit-Louis, aged twenty-four, has never had a chance to be anything but what he is—an unpleasing and unartful dodger, incapable of forging a letter in his native language correctly. Petit-Louis's idea of the good life is to lie in bed smoking gold-tipped cigarettes or to wander along the *plage* astonishing the young girls with his outfit. Like Viau, he is an amateur; unlike Viau, he is not a lone hand. He belongs to a gang of genuinely tough Marseillais for whom he acts as a decoy. Disliking him for himself and distrusting him as a loud-mouth, the gang successfully frame Petit-Louis for the murder of his elderly, infatuated protectress, a raddled, pathetic, middle-aged courtesan in semi-retirement. Constance Ropiquet, alias d'Orval, has old-world, *Belle-Epoque* pretensions, and pretensions—like all articles of bourgeois spiritual clothing—are, as we know, a red rag to Simenon. He treats poor Constance and her elderly lover, M. Parpin, whom she describes to Petit-Louis as an ex-diplomatist whereas in reality he is a retired customs official, with a sardonic wit and cruelty that is rare in his characterization, guying them with such savagery that one almost takes the old trot's part in the presiding judge's subsequent exchanges with Petit-Louis:

'When you first met Mme. Ropiquet, you realized straightaway what you stood to make out of this easy-circumstanced lady's unhappy passion for . . .'

'Mme. Ropiquet was a kept woman,' replied Petit-Louis, setting the score straight.

'Mme. Ropiquet was an honourable widow, whose only foible was to assume a high-sounding name, an innocent enough fantasy, surely . . .'

'Was it fantasy to take two thousand francs a month from an old man who has since killed himself?'

All to no avail. The crime reporters are already scribbling away ('. . . *le cynicisme incroyable de l'accusé qui . . .*'). Though Mme. Ropiquet's body has not yet been found—Petit-Louis, who discovered the dead woman, has in fact disposed of her remains in the harbour—the whole trial has been rigged and pre-judged from the start. To ensure conviction the police, acting in part-collusion with Petit-Louis's gang who have actually killed Mme. Ropiquet, have suppressed evidence, while the *juge d'instruction*, the harshest of all Simenon's judicial bureaucrats, has marshalled an army of witnesses ('*un cortège de personnes*') out of Petit-Louis's past to witness against his character from childhood onwards. The trial itself is one of Simenon's great court-room scenes, a scarifying set-piece that sticks in the reader's memory like a conglomerate and cumulative Daumier cartoon— or rather, as though the artist had achieved a drawing as thickly populated as one of Frith's canvases. The whole of Daumier is horribly and untranslatably present in

> . . . *la pose de l'assesseur de droite, un gros sanguin, qui se renversait en arrière, presque couché dans son fauteuil, et qui paraissait émerveillé d'être là, à sa place, de voir ce qu'il voyait, de vivre pareilles journées!*

If Simenon does belong, as Raymond Mortimer long ago claimed, 'to that great family of French moralists, ranging from Pascal and La Rochefoucauld to Flaubert and Mauriac, who are obsessed with the baseness of the human heart and the misery of the human situation', this side-glimpse of the legal *voyeur* on the Bench is a twentieth-, or any-, century Character from the pages of La Bruyère.

Objectively, *Cour d'Assises* might be described as a grim satire on the infernal machinery of human justice, the fact that 'law makes long spokes of the short stakes of men'. There is no light or shade in the book, no softening or redeeming feature in the characterization. If Constance Ropiquet and M. Parpin are no more than pathetic guys, Petit-Louis's mistress, mother and sister are all, in their different ways, equally odious and heartless.

Everything is hard, flat, deadpan, as metallic and resonant as the *Code* and the court procedure itself. The moralist's knowledge of the human heart, so compassionately present in *Au Bout du Rouleau*, is totally in abeyance here. Indeed, lodged at the heart of the matter, we have what might be described as a powerful Voltaire-Anatole France syndrome, effectively exercised again and again throughout the trial. Thus, attempting to lessen Petit-Louis's 'degree of responsibility', his defending counsel argues fatuously that if his client had not been the only conscript in his unit with sufficient muscular strength to perform the duties of regimental butcher, he might never have learned how to . . . Up jumps the Procureur-Général—'a little rosy-faced man with silk-white hair and double-comma moustaches'—crying 'with an indignation that was even perhaps sincere', 'Why not say at once that the French Army is responsible for this hideous butchery!' Here Simenon, the one-time objective reporter of the Stavisky trial—and the successor in this line to Gide, whose experiences as a juryman, related in his *Souvenirs de la Cour d'Assises*, emphasized the despairing imperfectibility rather than the active ill-intent of human justice—departs from his observer's role and gives his talent for the black comedy of indignation full rein. Petit-Louis may be no Calas or Dreyfus but his trial is no less of a travesty than theirs. By the time sentence is passed (twenty years' penal servitude instead of the guillotine, since in the case of this still undiscovered dead woman, the jury has magnanimously negatived the question of premeditation), the roles of accused and accusers have somehow been reversed. It is no longer Petit-Louis who is on trial but the judges, the jury, the lawyers, the witnesses, the journalists, the police, the society women-spectators and their well-groomed escorts. All of them suddenly find it urgently necessary to do something, anything, to go somewhere, anywhere, knowing that collectively they have done something that none of them can be proud of. As Petit-Louis goes down into the cells, a friendly policeman consoles him: 'Bah, you're young! You'll only be forty-five when you come out! What are you complaining about? . . .'

As we saw Sylvie, his father and the others follow Viau to the cemetery, similarly, in the haunting last chapter of *Le Locataire*,

Elie Nagéar's sister from Istanbul and his landlady, Mme. Baron, the railwayman's wife, who has come what is for her a much further way from Charleroi, strain to follow Elie with their eyes as he and his batch of fellow-convicts are embarked for the penal settlements. Watching from far off, unknown to each other, the one in the press launch, the other from the shore of the Ile de Ré, the two women strive to pick Elie out among the mass of blurred faces on the deck of the prison transport. No one follows Petit-Louis in spirit or in the flesh. Of all Simenon's unfortunates, he is perhaps the most human because he is the weakest and the most alone.

Chapter 6

AN IMPRESSION OF ISHMAELIA
PART II

TALKING to Simenon at Epalinges and remarking on Maigret's difficulties and tussles with the various *juges d'instruction* that he works with, Coméliau, Amadieu and the rest, I asked him if his personal opinion of the magistrature was as severe as his fiction indicated. His reply was vigorous and uncompromising—'*Je déteste cette assurance!*' And not only magistrates, one gathered, but most human beings dressed in executive authority, particularly generals and colonial officials. (Though military men are almost non-existent in Simenon's repertory, the colonial satrapy is well-represented, not only in *Touriste de Bananes* but in *Le Blanc à Lunettes* [1937] and in that vivid equatorial nightmare *Le Coup de Lune* [1933].) Though we shall be returning to this pair of novels later, it is worth remarking in parenthesis that much of Simenon's basic attitude to colonial Africa and Oceania is to be found in *L'Aventure*, a fascinating and little-known discourse that he delivered in 1937 on the publication of *Le Testament Donadieu*.[1] As is well known, the French legal profession is divided into two branches, the ascending grades of the magistrature being entirely separate from the art of advocacy; in this it is unlike the English system where noted silks are elevated to the Bench. Two uninterchangeable types of mind result from this division and both are depicted with the same skilful, though different and unequal malice in Simenon's fiction. On the whole the Bench fares better than the Bar. As a general run, Simenon's

[1] Reprinted in Vol. 8: *Oeuvres Complètes de Georges Simenon*, Ed. Gilbert Sigaux, Editions Rencontre, 1967. To this *conférence* might be applied the phrase 'firm but rambling', coined by Mr. Kenneth Tynan to describe the manner in which a principal witness gave evidence in the *Lady Chatterley's Lover* case in 1959.

barristers are a shallow lot—socially and materially ambitious, especially when practising in the provinces, airily callous in respect of their clients and obligations, quick on cheap points of rhetoric, slow on psychology. Maître Fagonet of *La Veuve Couderc*, even more Maître Abeille of *Les Rescapés du 'Télémaque'*, are excellent examples of their kind. The latter novel, an extraordinary tale of Norman fisher-folk, though it originates in an act of cannibalism on the high seas, is really concerned with Charles Canut's attempt to prove his brother innocent of murder. It is particularly rich in its description of Old Father Antick busy at his tricks of postponement and frustration. Simenon's detestation of *l'assurance* in all its forms is only equalled by his fury at the way in which decent, humble folk cringe respectfully before officialdom. (This feeling can be traced directly back to Elise and to Roger's childhood, as described in *Pedigree*. Here at least Parinaud's thesis has been amply vindicated.) Canut, a simple working-man, makes his way through the law courts of Rouen like a somnambulist who has strayed out of the first chapter of *Bleak House* into the world of Kafka. Thus it comes as no surprise that when Pierre Canut's innocence is eventually established, it is in no way thanks to the efforts of Superintendent Gentil's police officers or to Canut's legal advisers, but solely to his brother's devotion and perseverance.

As though to make amends to a profession that he normally portrays in the most cursory and unflattering light, Simenon has created two advocates, poles apart in temperament, each of whom is the hero (using that word for once in a general and unspecifically Simenonian sense) of a remarkable novel, the one a tragi-comic melodrama, the other a genuine tragedy of infatuation.

Les Inconnus dans la Maison (1940) has been described as a brilliant treatment of adolescent tensions and the misunderstanding or lack of communication between bourgeois generations in a French provincial town as the result of a murder. In fact, though this discovery of a corpse does provide the main plot and action of the novel, its real theme is the secluded character of Hector Loursat himself and his re-emergence as an active human being at the moment of crisis.

Loursat is, to all intents and purposes, a widower and a recluse. Ever since his wife left him umpteen years ago, he has cut himself off from the world and from his practice at the Bar and shut himself up in a wing of his huge family house at Moulins, taking his meals with his daughter Nicole and waited on by a spiteful old servant named Josephine, known as 'The Dwarf'. Behind the padded baize door of his part of the house, he exploits his patrimony, drinking four or more bottles of Burgundy a day and devouring, in desultory fashion, the contents of his enormous library.

Loursat is an intellectual beachcomber of the first order. One might say that he is the only genuine and disinterested intellectual to be found in Simenon's works, certainly the only one to receive genuinely favourable treatment. Admirers of *Ceux de la Soif* may object that Professor Hermann Müller, the platonic nudist and island-recluse of the Galapagos, is a genuine intellectual. Indeed, one might describe him as a cruel but effective parody of the type—the kind of puritanical, dried-up materialist (or, in terms of today, behaviourist) who turns up so often, only to be guyed, in Chesterton's Father Brown stories. In the contrast that exists between his fiercely penetrating mind and his wasting brain-sick body, the Berlin professor might be taken to be a fictional caricature of Nietzsche (one of the few writers Müller really admires). Yet, as his fantastic relationship with Magdalena, his devoted disciple, proves, Müller is too arrogantly self-conscious to be self-sufficient; as a result, Simenon treats him with the contempt that he reserves for all human beings who are anti-life without sufficient reason. Whereas, though Loursat lives entirely to and for himself, and his bear-like exterior and boorish behaviour is far from prepossessing, Simenon extends him the sympathy that he gives freely to all those of his characters who have proved their self-sufficiency—whose solitariness, in other words, is as active, wilfully cheerful and self-chosen as that of Kipling's cat. Indeed, despite his domestic tragedy of long ago (which in fact hardly seems to bother the retired pleader one whit) the reader has a sneaking suspicion that Simenon envies Loursat in the same way as he envies Bouvet. Both, in their different ways, belong to that '*salon des ratés*' or Other Club of the Unconcerned that faces and complements Simenon's rival establishment of tragic heroes across the street:

It [Loursat's stove] roared away, turning red in no time at all, and now and then Loursat would go up to it as if it were a good dog, throw friendly shovelfuls of coke into its mouth, and squat down to poke it.

The slow train to Montluçon had gone. Another train whistled above the town, but this time it was just a goods train. A film was flickering on the screen for the benefit of a few people scattered about the cinema, which smelt of wet clothing. The Prefect led his guests into the smoking-room and opened a box of cigars.

. . . Loursat blew his nose, in the way old men and peasants do, first of all unfolding his handkerchief completely, making a noise like a trumpet three, four, five times, and then folding the handkerchief up again just as meticulously. He was alone in his overheated lair whose door he locked from inclination, though Nicole said it was from vice.

His grey hair was naturally bushy and he made it untidier by running his fingers through it like a comb. His beard was vaguely pointed, and his moustache had a brownish-yellow tinge from the cigarettes he smoked.

There were cigarette-ends everywhere, on the floor and in the ashtrays, on the stove and on the bindings of the books.

Smoking a cigarette, Loursat lumbered across the room to pick up the bottle warming in one corner of the fireplace.

Cars went by along the Rue de Paris, several blocks away, with windscreen-wipers working, rain driving against the headlamps, and pale faces inside.

Loursat did nothing, let his cigarette go out, lit it again, and spat the end out anywhere, while his hand reached for a book and opened it at random.

Then he read a little, took a few sips of wine, hummed to himself, crossed his legs and uncrossed them again. There were books piled up as high as the ceiling. And more books in the corridors, in most of the rooms of the house: books which belonged to him, and others dating back to his father or his grandfather.

For no particular reason, he planted himself in front of one bookcase, possibly forgot where he was, and smoked a whole cigarette before seizing a volume, which he took to his desk like a puppy taking a crust to bury under the straw in its kennel.

This had been going on for twenty years, or eighteen to be precise, and during that time no one had ever got him to dine out, neither the Rogissarts, who were his cousins and gave a dinner-party followed by bridge every Friday, nor the president of the local bar council who had been a close friend of his father, nor his brother-in-law Dossin, who was fond of entertaining politicians, nor finally the successive Prefects, who, on their arrival, didn't know the situation and sent him an invitation.

He scratched himself, grunted, coughed, blew his nose, spat. He was hot. His smoking-jacket was covered with fine ash. He read ten pages of a legal treatise and straight afterwards opened, at the middle, some seventeenth-century memoirs.

As the hours went by, he became drowsier, his eyes grew more and more watery, and his gestures took on an almost hieratical slowness.

. . . He could hear the raindrops, and now and then the creak of a shutter which had not been properly secured. The wind was rising and sudden gusts blew along the streets. He could also hear, as regular as a metronome, the ticking of his gold watch in his waistcoat pocket.

He had re-read a few pages of the *Voyage of Tamerlane* which smelt of old paper and whose binding was crumbling. He was probably about to get up and look for something else to read when he slowly raised his head, puzzled and surprised.

. . . The sound which had just roused Loursat from his stupor was new and completely unusual.

The sound is in fact the shot that has killed the injured criminal whom Nicole and her gang of teenagers have been sheltering and concealing in the other wing of her father's town house. All, except for Nicole's lover, Emile, are the children of the most respectable well-to-do citizens of Moulins. Needless to say, Emile, a poor widow's son and the latest recruit to Nicole's 'wrong set', is charged with the man's murder. Loursat assumes his defence and wins a resounding acquittal. The young people marry and go to live in Paris and the advocate returns to his books and his wine cellar.

As a *scène de la vie de province*, the novel is effective melodrama on roughly the same level as *Les Fantômes du Chapelier*, though without the hatter's fiendish ingenuity and Sim's own ingenious construction. Nicole and her boy-friends are conventional tearaways and, except for the circumstances surrounding them, are uninteresting in themselves, as tiresome to the reader as to their parents and relations. It is surprising that Simenon, who writes so well about children, seldom seems able to handle adolescents—or even young people generally—with the same perceptiveness and individuality. Brash, nervous, headstrong, secretive—they all seem to have come indiscriminately out of a common mould. It is this, among its other shortcomings, that makes *Les Soeurs Lacroix* (1938) such a rare failure, almost a positive embarrassment, as a novel. It is not only the two sisters or Germaine's husband Jules but the children themselves who are so incredible and unconvincing. As an exposure of the provincial *foyer clos* this unreal tale of skeletons in the family cupboard—executed for once without any narrative assistance from Sim—reads like a bad pastiche of Mauriac.

Reverting to Loursat himself, the temptation to elevate him to the rank of Simenon's opters-out of life or would-be escapers—to an equality with Bouvet or Maugin, say—must be resisted. Narcejac, in his study of the writer, mistakenly declares that Loursat is despised by his neighbours whereas Simenon makes it very clear early in the novel that, however anti-social his behaviour, his connections and his great talents (that is, when he chooses to employ them) combine to make Loursat a figure of awe and grudging admiration among the Moulins bourgeoisie. (The habitual reader of Simenon comes in time to realize that, at the humdrum un-tragic level of day-to-day life, the writer has his own brand of high bourgeois snobbery. Loursat, with his *noblesse de robe* background, is among the Republic's patricians.) However effective as a character, Hector Loursat is essentially one-dimensional and theatrical—a bear with a heart of gold, as much of the theatre as the good-hearted martinet-hero of the late Roger Ferdinand's famous stock comedy *Le Président Haudecoeur*. From this point of view Loursat can be regarded as a touchstone or catalyst, an instrument useful in determining the nature or specific gravity of any of his creator's productions. As we have insisted all along, the range of moods and modes that Simenon makes use of in his fiction is as extensive as the variety of his milieux, the fertility of his plots and situations and the range of his repertory of character. If it is perverse and almost impossible to class him as a mere entertainer, even in the earliest of the Maigret series, neither can he be considered always 'wholly serious' in the rest of his fiction. Each of the novels must be judged according to the intention that inspired it—as tragedy, tragi-comedy, melodrama, black farce, nightmare or what you will.

Thus *En cas de malheur* (1956) is wholly serious throughout, a study of infatuation on the classic lines of *Manon Lescaut*, though its hero is very different in age and status to Des Grieux—indeed, at an un-existential level and in terms of the Civil Register, he corresponds closely to the hero of Camus's *La Chute*. At forty-five Lucien Gobillot is a top pleader of the Paris criminal bar—rich, famous, fashionable, unscrupulous, repulsively ugly ('my famous toad's face') and comfortably married to his *mondaine* understanding ex-mistress, herself the wife of his former chief. Into this worldly bed of roses comes Yvette, a waif-prostitute in distress, involved in a Montparnasse hold-up (as the journalists put it: 'If you're innocent, take any good lawyer. If you're guilty, get in touch with Maître Gobillot'):

> My visitor's face was harshly lighted by the lamp trained on the confessional chair, and I remember my distress when I analysed it, for it was a child's face and a very old face at the same time, a mixture of *naiveté* and deceit; of innocence and vice, I would like to add, except that I don't like those words, which I reserve for juries.
>
> She was thin, physically run down, like girls of her age who live unhealthy lives in Paris. What made me think she probably had dirty feet?
>
> 'Is there a charge against you?'
>
> 'There's certainly going to be.'

Brazenly rigging the case, Gobillot secures Yvette's acquittal. In the outcome, he falls in love with his client. Not that he would put it like that:

> More often I've slept with girls, professional or non-professional, and when I think about it, I realize that they all had certain things in common with Yvette, which had escaped me until now.
>
> My strongest impulse was probably a craving for pure sex, if I can use that expression without raising a smile, I mean sex without any considerations of emotion or passion. Let's say sex in its raw state. Or its cynical state.
>
> . . . But I can't be with Yvette for an hour without feeling an urge to see her nakedness, to touch her, to ask her to caress me.
>
> Tomorrow it's possible that I may think and write the opposite, but I doubt it. For me Yvette, like most of the girls who have meant anything to me, personifies the female, with her weaknesses, her

cowardice, and also with her instinct to cling to the male and make herself his slave.

I remember her surprise and pride the day I slapped her face, and since then she has sometimes driven me to the breaking-point just to see me do it again.

I don't claim that she loves me. I don't want anything to do with that word.

But she has renounced being herself. She has placed her fate in my hands. No matter if it is out of laziness or lack of initiative. It's her role, and I see, perhaps naively, a symbol in the way she once spread her thighs apart on the corner of my desk, after asking me to defend her.

. . . She tells lies. She's deceitful. She puts on acts. She makes up stories to worry me and, now that she's sure of her daily bread, she wallows in laziness; there are days when she hardly gets out of bed, keeping the television switched on at the foot of it.

Later, the knowledge that Yvette is pregnant changes and deepens Lucien's feelings for her. A new and sober happiness, quite alien to his character and unlike anything he has previously known, is awakened in him. But Gobillot is one of nature's Cartesians, a man who, for all his professionally notorious falsities and gimmicks, is completely honest with himself. And because, for the first time in his life perhaps, he is unable to analyse his feelings, he is disquieted. Meanwhile, he prepares to take Yvette on a ski-ing holiday. Sudden death cuts short his obsession. Yvette's other lover, a young workman named Mazetti, stabs her to death in a fit of jealousy, and Gobillot, having completed his personal dossier for use 'in case of misfortune', hands it over to Mazetti's defence counsel, resolving that 'as for me, I'll go on defending the real scum'.

Set down baldly like this, *En cas de malheur* sounds like a conventional *crime passionel* melodrama. Though the book is less than 160 pages, it abounds in sub-plot, flash-back and accessory characters: Gobillot's wife Viviane and her political salon world; her first husband, the distinguished *bâtonnier* (deceived or not, when he was first cuckolded so long ago?); Gobillot's curious father; and Janice, the pretty, sympathetic maid-companion, devotedly maternal but quite un-lesbian, whom Gobillot instals in Yvette's flat. All these elements provide an enveloping surround to the obsessive centre of the novel.

One of the great drawbacks to interpreting Simenon's fiction successfully in terms of conventional criticism of the novel is that where everything—persons, places, actions, gestures—is made so immediate and photographic (cinematic, one should say, perhaps), so overwhelmingly *present* to the reader's eye, the reflective imagination is liable to go by default. The kind of critical rationale that presupposes what might be loosely called a writer's philosophy of life or reality—the rationale that one can apply to, say, a novel by George Eliot or Conrad or Henry James—is correspondingly difficult if not impossible in the case of Simenon, where everything that is needful to the development of the tragedy is given and little or no margin for moral speculation is provided.

Because the best of Simenon's work stems from his own striking and original conception of contemporary tragedy rather than from the assumptions of the nineteenth- and twentieth-century novel, the old aesthetic precept of 'in the subjective element immerse' is inapplicable in his case. At the risk of repeating what has been said already, it must be emphasized that the creative root of his matter is to be found in Greek drama rather than in the novel proper. In one sense the huge body of his work might be figuratively described as a repeopling of the House of Atreus, the invasion of Thebes and Tauris and Mycenae by the *petits-gens* of Liège and Montparnasse and Poitiers, or, as in this novel, the smart, brittle society of the Île St. Louis and the soiled, shabby corridors of the Palais de Justice.

There is nothing subjective in Simenon. There is, however, much that is mysterious and sphinx-like. In the case of *En cas de malheur* it discloses itself early on in the book when Gobillot encounters his friend, the politician Moriat, at a party:

> At Corine's, Moriat doesn't pose for the benefit of his constituents or posterity. He shows himself as he is, and he often looks to me like a man who is bored or more precisely a man who is trying to come up to expectations.
>
> On Sunday, the first time our eyes met, he was watching me and wrinkling his brow as if he was discovering in me a new element, something I'm tempted to call a sign.
>
> I wouldn't like to repeat aloud what I'm about to write, out of shame and for fear of being ridiculous, but that Sunday I began to

believe in the sign, an invisible mark that can only be discerned by the initiated, by those who bear it themselves.

Am I going to think this through to the end? Only special people can have that sign, people who have lived a lot, seen a lot, tried everything for themselves, above all, people who have made an abnormal effort, reached or almost reached their goal, and I don't think you can acquire it under a certain age, the middle forties, say. . . .

Yet I don't think he is ambitious, or else, if he once was, in a petty childish way, he isn't any more. He submits to his fate, his personality, just as some actors are condemned to play the same role all their lives.

Paradoxically, it is the great actor Maugin's refusal to submit to fate and his own personality that is the theme of *Les Volets Verts*—a typical example of Sim's ingenious ability to vary, complement or retort upon Simenon's parcel of basic situations. Moriat, the politician, the unwilling conformist, drinks himself into near-insensibility without pleasure at Corine's in order to maintain his public *persona*: Maugin's excesses are the complementary result of his need to discover his real nature as a human-being, the essential Maugin that lies outside or beneath the public role he has assumed, and to answer the sphinx's riddle of his own personality.

It would be possible—and not altogether fanciful—to propound a chemical classification of Simenon's fiction in terms of complementary opposites. Thus, for example, one might bracket *Dimanche* (1959) with *L'Escalier de Fer* (1953), *Le Coup de Lune* (1933) with *Le Blanc à Lunettes* (1937), *La Fuite de Monsieur Monde* (1946) with *L'Enterrement de Monsieur Bouvet* (1950), and so on. In the case of the first pair, each a remarkable novel in its own right, both are flawed by their respective conclusions— the first by a brilliant *volte-face* ending worthy of a Maupassant or a Maugham long short story but quite inadequate in this case considering what has gone before, the second by a Gordian knot stroke of what I would call the artificially 'sacrificial' psychology all too familiar to readers of Simenon but freshly and infuriatingly 'out of true' each time it occurs—an adult, pseudo-sophisticated variant of the old penny-dreadful, 'at a bound Sexton Blake freed himself' serial technique. It is in this connection that we remember Brigid Brophy's wise words about the 'top-heaviness' of much of Simenon's fiction, the 'over-loading of the first third of the book' and the endings that don't manage to 'make quite the decisive home-coming click of surprise and inevitability'.

The first forty pages of *Dimanche* describe how Emile, a Breton peasant's son, arrives at the position of being chef of a small hotel near Nice and the married chattel of Berthe, its proprietress:

> 'I presume,' Madame Harnaud [Berthe's mother] went on after a silence, 'that the two of you intend to draw up a marriage contract?'
> It was then that Berthe had raised her head and looked at Emile with a look he was never to forget, before saying quietly, with a faint tremor of her lips:
> 'No.'
> The mother was taken in, imagined it to be generosity on the part of her daughter, or the blindness of love. The proof is that she had countered, not without a touch of irritation:
> 'I know what one feels when one is young. All the same, one must look a little further, for none of us can foresee the future.'
> Berthe had repeated firmly:
> 'We do not need a contract.'
> He could not have said by exactly what mechanism these words constituted a sort of act of possession of his person. Had not Berthe bought him, much more safely and surely than by any contract duly signed and sealed?

Fifty pages further on, Emile, having realized that his wife has taken away his pride and decided to murder her, begins to fall in love with the crime itself. 'He had more and more the conviction that he was undergoing an exceptional experience . . . Unfortunately there was only himself to watch himself living.' In the event—a *tour de force* of Sim as storyteller—the reader, who has watched Emile so closely as to have become identified with him, is left feeling cheated. It is as if, at the moment of catharsis, Simenon had swerved aside. Certainly we receive a shock, but it is a shock of disappointment with the author's misplaced ingenuity rather than a genuine shudder at the conclusion of the novel itself.

Dimanche is the tale of a man who plans to murder his wife. In *L'Escalier de Fer* a timid, middle-aged husband is led to the grim discovery that his wife is slowly poisoning him with arsenic in order to marry her young lover. Here again the psychology is masterly, the situation being wonderfully heightened by Etienne's realization that Louise (one of Simenon's prize Clytemnestras) is disposing of him in the same way as, years before, she disposed of her first husband Guillaume in the interests of their own love affair:

> He was not outraged. He had always known that, sooner or later, something terrible would happen; it was, he felt, no more than he deserved. He had kept silent that other time, knowing all the facts, and, even though some things had never been put into words, he was just as guilty as Louise.
> In answering 'yes', when a certain question was put to him, he had pronounced Guillaume's death sentence.
> The years during which they had been together were merely a breathing space. They had lived accordingly, waiting, waiting, year after year, and in those years he had felt the need, an increasingly agonizing need, to lose himself in Louise, to become one with her, because it was for this that the thing had been done; it was their only excuse, if any excuse were admissible.
> And it was for this same reason that she, as much as he, had fiercely warded off any intrusion into their lives by other people.

Yet here again, having created this state of tension, Simenon arbitrarily ends it with Etienne's banal and 'sacrificial' suicide.

In the case of the African pair, *Le Blanc à Lunettes* and *Le Coup de Lune*, these strictures do not apply. The first might be described as a drama of manners (perhaps tragi-comedy would be a better description). An expert piece of story-telling, its plot revolves round one of Simenon's rare and genuine heroes— Ferdinand Graux, a French coffee planter in the Belgian Congo, first glimpsed returning from home leave in company with a rather dreadful couple, the Bodets. Georges, the husband, is a young junior official, potentially a heavy drinker, running to seed. He has spent his first leave getting married to Yette, a shrill, vulgar, excitable, fundamentally good-hearted Parisian girl of not more than twenty, born to be a banal scourge to herself and whatever society she finds herself in. At this outset level, the book reads like an expansion of one of Maugham's Ashenden stories.

> She was young, not more than twenty, and had the rather washed-out complexion of the city-bred girl. On board ship she seemed pathetically out of place, and spent her days hunting round for congenial company. Her husband, who had already got into white

drill suits, passed most of his time playing belote. The more select
coterie on board took no notice of her, and played bridge from morn
till bed-time.

Obviously she resented being 'out of it', and she paced the decks
indefatigably, buttonholing stewards and ship's officers. On the
fourth night out she badgered the purser into getting up an after-
dinner dance on deck. When it began, Graux retreated to his cabin.

Poor Yette has her time-wasting counterpart in almost every
novel of life aboard ship that Simenon has ever written. Graux,
polite, self-contained, solitary-minded, dedicated to his work in
Africa, his one desire to be left in peace, treats Yette, who attaches
herself to him like a limpet, with more consideration than her
creator who, having used the Bodets to comic introductory effect
and to offset his hero's businesslike serenity, gets rid of them in a
somewhat brutal and perfunctory fashion later in the book.
Like most of the other characters, all rendered in Simenon's
ineffable shorthand—Major Crosby, the genial ex-Edwardian
clubman, turned elephant breeder; Baligi, Graux's pathetic
teenage native mistress; and the terrible Costermans couple who
drive Georges to suicide and Yette to despair—the Bodets are
there to quicken the narrative pace. The reader has the feeling
that contractor Sim has worked their story in to fit the specifica-
tions of the architectural situation as a whole—a situation that
is not only psychological but (something that is much rarer in
this writer's work) has a profoundly Simenonian moral adhering
to it.

On getting home Graux learns that a private aeroplane containing
a young married Englishwoman and a playboy friend of hers,
acting as pilot, has made a forced landing on his estate. Lady
Mary Mackinson, blonde, patrician, and conventionally un-
conventional, a beauty of the type long ago made famous by
Gladys Cooper, having damaged Graux's plantation, proceeds to
make havoc with his peace of mind. After a quick, fugitive tumble
in his bungalow and a good deal of clipped, inconclusive conversation, she leaves lightheartedly for home and Graux, no
longer the self-sufficient man of quality but a prey to complete
infatuation, follows her.

Meanwhile, before this point in the book has been reached,

the whole atmosphere of the novel, its pace, psychology, characters' motivation—the very degree of reality that, as it were, attaches to it—has subtly changed. The transition takes place back in Moulins, Ferdinand's home town, in the space of eight pages. Emmeline, Ferdinand's fiancée, a grave, beautiful, thoughtful young woman, his ideal wife and the perfect complement to his own innate seriousness, alarmed by his letters, decides to fly out to the Congo at once. In the event, tragedy is avoided. Ferdinand, by an act of will, dissolves his fantasy. He and Emmeline begin their new life—a partnership based on trust, affection and mutual respect—in the Africa of their choice: an Africa impersonal in its mystery and prosaic in its challenges, a continent where rains and droughts, pest, diseases and unremitting struggle will, so the final page of the book implies, drown and swallow up the image of Ferdinand's single and exoteric infatuation.

As barely sketched in this way, *Le Blanc à Lunettes* seems little more than a tropical variant of Noël Coward's *Brief Encounter* with the sexes reversed and a measure of hard lighthearted sophistication thrown in. Yet when Lady Mary and Captain Phelps, her attendant cavalier, Major Crosby, Baligi, Camille (Graux's French assistant), the Bodets, the Costermans and the rest of the excellently realized cast have been discarded, Ferdinand and Emmeline remain tranquilly secure in our imagination. They belong to that highly select group in the vast Simenonian repertoire who have managed to avoid the pit that their creator has so carefully dug for them. In case this last sentence appears fanciful and, in view of what has been written about the scrupulous and hyper-detailed planning that goes into a Simenon novel— the manila envelope dossiers of characters and settings, with grandparents on both sides and every room in a house accounted for, whether the novel is to make use of them or not—it must be emphasized again that Simenon rarely or never plans the *plot* of a novel in advance, but only the situation. In this—as in two other startling respects, namely his lack of any general philosphy of life and his abiding interest in the obsessional—he may be said to resemble Trollope (of all writers!), whose objection to the art of Wilkie Collins was precisely that,

. . . when I sit down to write a novel I do not at all know, and I do not very much care, how it is to end. Wilkie Collins seems so to construct his that he not only, before writing, plans everything on paper, down to the minutest detail, from the beginning to the end; then plots it all back again, to see that there is no piece of necessary dovetailing which does not dovetail with absolute accuracy.

Admittedly the outcome of a Trollope novel, in the context of the writer's known moral code and psychological standpoint, is foreseeable, or at least can be prophesied with a high degree of probability. If Trollope, as Walter Allen has pointed out, has no general philosophy of life, he has 'a strong shrewd grasp of right and wrong in social behaviour', an angle of vision directed from his own time and place in the English nineteenth century. Simenon has no such predilections. Insofar as any artist can be unconditioned, he is the most determinedly unconditioned writer of our time: classless, in the literary sense that he is negatively or disinterestedly anti-bourgeois and that the novel, from any point of view, sociological, aesthetic or otherwise, is still the purest bourgeois art form in existence; stateless in his own sense that by being born a Belgian citizen he can claim to be 'without nationality'; and entirely unmetaphysical, without any epistemology or theory of human ends and means. His only loyalty is to his own imagination—to the vast mythology of private destinies over which he arbitrarily and autonomously presides, spinning the fates of each, striking or releasing at his will or as the hidden lines, the undiscovered ends of their character, direct.

For Graux, once Lady Mary has been exorcised from his imagination, the Congo is as bracing as proverbial Skegness. For young Joseph Timar, the ill-fated hero of *Le Coup de Lune*, Africa is an upas-tree that spells disaster. Dumped down on the coast of French Equatoria, gauche, friendless, a less than average young man, he falls easy prey to Adèle, his hotel proprietress, a predatory and experienced older woman. They get married and she sells the hotel in order to further her pet commercial project. This involves sending the pair of them up-river where drink, fever and his lack of will quickly effect Timar's destruction. In the tragedy that follows, Adèle is herself destroyed (a rare case of Simenon displaying a change of heart in regard to a woman's character) and Timar is shipped home to France, under supervision—very like Captain Bassot in *45° à l'Ombre*. As in the case of the Captain, his hallucinatory state is ambiguous:

> With a faint hiss the bows cut through the grey-blue smoothness. The smoke-room verandah was in shadow. A sailor was giving a fresh coat of red paint to the interior of the wind-scoops.
>
> Timar resolved to make himself agreeable. With Blanche, with everyone at La Rochelle and La Pallice. He'd come to the wharf to see the liners bound for Africa, watch young men and Civil Servants going on board.
>
> But he wouldn't say anything. Not a word. Only once in a while, at night, he'd have his moon-stroke—an 'attack' they would call it— and once again would feel his senses swooning in the sultry air and, in a waking dream, see Adèle's pale form glimmering in the bed beside him—while his wife in her nightdress warmed up a potion on the spirit-lamp.
>
> People still stared at him uneasily as he walked by. He felt so calm, his brain was working now so smoothly, with such logical precision, that he couldn't resist the temptation of mystifying them a bit, playing to the gallery. With twinkling, fever-bright eyes he watched their faces as he said out loud: 'But there's no such place as Africa.'

The descriptive background of the flora—and colonial human fauna—of the book is superb, reminding the reader strongly of Conrad's *The Heart of Darkness*, though the resemblance ends with the *mise-en-scène*. Its real centre is the strong-willed (and as it turns out, strong-hearted) Adèle, the coastal Jocasta turned victim, rather than the ineffectual Timar.

Emile and Etienne are examples of situations in reverse, Graux and Timar pair off naturally enough. In a different way again, one could bracket the two Elies of *Le Locataire* (1934) and *Crime Impuni* (1954), not for anything similar or opposite in their characters but as examples of the skilful way in which Simenon has in each case varied their common background—the Belgian boarding-house and its inmates that basically belong to *Pedigree*. (The two murderers——the flamboyant Turkish Elie and his secretive Ashkenazi counterpart—do, in fact, complement each other admirably.)

Finally, we have two contrasted examples of a theme dear to Simenon's heart, the flight or *fugue*. In the case of the first (*La Fuite de Monsieur Monde*, 1946), what begins as an escape ends

as a return to reality. M. Monde, a prosperous Parisian businessman, disgusted with the homosexual goings-on of his son and
tired of his shrewish, nagging second wife, decides to take leave
of his family. He draws 300,000 francs from his bank (having
left, he imagines, Mme. Monde with power of attorney), and
decamps to Marseilles. Lying in his hotel bedroom on the first
night of his freedom, he ponders his life, feeling 'like a great
caryatid released, at long last, from its burden':

> 'Why have you treated me so harshly?' he longed to whisper in
> the sea's ear.
> He had tried so hard to do the right thing. He had married so as
> to have a home and children, he had wanted to be a fruitful, not a
> sterile, tree; and one morning his wife had left him; he had found
> himself with a baby in one cot, a small girl in the other, without
> understanding, without knowing; he had been in despair, and those
> whom he questioned had smiled at his innocence; and finally, in
> forgotten drawers, he had discovered horrible drawings, obscene
> photographs, unspeakable things which had revealed to him the true
> nature of the woman he had thought so guileless.
> . . . He stretched out his whole frame in deep relief, and the little
> shining waves came up to lick the sand by his side; perhaps one of
> them would soon reach him for a caress.

Later he meets Julie, a young night-club hostess whose lover
has deserted her. She accepts him as her protector (drolly at
first but later with real affection) and together they move to Nice.
Here M. Monde's nest-egg is stolen and the pair are forced to
take employment in a local *boîte*, she in her old job, he as a kitchen
supervisor. In the night-club M. Monde encounters his first wife,
ex-companion to a dead millionairess, now a pauper and a hopeless
heroin-addict. In rescuing and reclaiming Thérèse, he completes
the circle of his flight and returns to his family, relaxed, a new man,
'part of life, as flexible and fluid as life itself':

> Every week, or almost, Julie would write to him on headed note-
> paper from Gerly's or Le Monico. She told him news of Monsieur
> René, of Charlotte, of all his acquaintances. And he would answer her.
> Boucard [his doctor], meanwhile, talked to him every evening at
> the Cintra about Thérèse, who longed to see him again.
> 'You ought to go there once, at least.'
> 'What's the use?'
> 'Just imagine, she believed that it was for her sake that you . . .'

S.I.C.—9

Monsieur Monde looked him quite calmly in the eyes. 'And so?'
'She was dreadfully disappointed.'
'Oh!'
And Boucard desisted, probably because like everyone else he was
deeply impressed by this man who had laid all ghosts, who had lost
all shadows, and who stared you in the eyes with cold serenity.

M. Monde's flight brings him back, a changed human being,
to the point from which he started. In the case of René Bouvet,
the flight is a genuine *fugue*, the purest of Simenon's escapist
fantasies. On a bright Parisian summer's morning, old M. Bouvet,
in his straw hat and creamy linen jacket, is engaged in his favourite
form of serendipity, examining the bookstalls on the *quais*.
Suddenly he heels over, scattering a portfolio of prints, and falls
to the pavement. An American student snaps the dead man with
his Leica, triggering off a strange tragi-comedy of false identities.
Mme. Jeanne, the devoted concierge, lays the old man out on the
bed in his lodgings, cuts a sprig of box, lights candles and sends
a small boy out for holy water. Soon M. Bouvet has his first round
of visitors—including an enormous moon-faced old woman who
says nothing but just stares and departs, leaving a small bunch
of violets, and a Mrs. Marsh (hard-faced, well-dressed and wearing
a lot of jewellery), who identifies the dead man by a scar on his
leg and declares: 'He is my husband, Samuel Marsh, of Ouagi
Mines.'

Thus Bouvet is stripped of the first layer of his aliases. Further
police enquiries are entrusted to M. Beaupère—one of Simenon's
classic policemen, a quasi-Dickensian creation, lugubrious, con-
scientious, pathetic:

> He was the only detective in the Quai des Orfèvres who was never
> called by his name without adding the 'Monsieur', perhaps because
> of his age, his sad dignity of an old and trusted employee who has
> his burdens and his cares.
>
> He was dressed in black in the month of August, and perhaps
> he was in mourning again, perhaps he was simply wearing out his
> mourning suit from the time before.
>
> He had so closely identified himself with the 'investigations under-
> taken on behalf of the families concerned' that they would not have
> dreamed of confiding one of these cases to anyone else . . .
>
> The thing that helped him, that had helped him all his life, was
> that he never felt he was on a wild-goose chase. What if he was

only a little wheel in the police machine? He had such a respect for it that this respect lent colour to his own personality and to his every act and gesture. His wife helped him when she spoke of him to people as 'My husband, the detective'.

M. Beaupère's patient investigations lead him to interrogate Félix Legalle, Bouvet's quay-side crony, a one-time school-teacher whom drink has turned into a *clochard*. Mumblingly, as though talking to himself, taking swigs at the litre bottle that the old detective has thoughtfully provided, 'the Professor' tells of his friendship with the strange old gentleman who wasn't interested in money but 'talked like somebody who'd once been rich':

> 'It's not easy to explain, and I'm not sure. He asked me questions. He watched me, watched the others . . .'
> 'What others?'
> 'The others like me.'
> 'What did he want to find out?'
> 'Whether it was hard, whether sometimes I didn't want to lead some other kind of life . . . How they treated us on the Salvation Army barge . . . Whether it was true that sometimes the police beat us up . . . I don't know . . . It's complicated . . . I'm not used to it any more . . . I got the idea that he'd have liked to come . . .'
> 'Where?'
> 'With us. And still I may be mistaken. It's because of his questions. And also because it was always he that was running after me. Some-times he'd wait for me for an hour or longer . . .'
> 'Where?'
> 'On the Place Maubert, or anywhere . . .'

Eventually—through his ex-business partner, his widowed sister and, above all, through the white-haired moon-faced Mlle. Blanche, his mistress of forty years before—the whole astonishing life of Gaston Lamblot, alias Marsh, alias Bouvet is unmasked. To faithful Mme. Jeanne's delight, the police return her lodger's body and he is given Christian burial. The description of M. Bouvet's funeral procession is one of Simenon's perfect endings—no question of the home-coming click of inevitability not working on this occasion:

> In the last carriage they all hesitated to lean back on the cushions and make themselves comfortable. Mademoiselle Blanche was no longer crying.

'Who would think that he was living so close by and I didn't know,' she sighed. 'I could have run into him in the street. It's true he wouldn't have recognized me, and maybe he wouldn't have wanted to see me again.'

Then Madame Jeanne flashed the Professor a knowing look. Because after all, even though they were the last in the procession, they were about the only ones Monsieur Bouvet expected to have at his funeral.

He hadn't run away from them. He had come to them. He had chosen them.

The old tramp's eyes were sparkling even more than the concierge's. He alone knew by how narrow a margin Monsieur Bouvet hadn't run away one more time, hadn't come to search him out at the Place Maubert or on the *quais* . . .

A red lorry passed them, fell into the procession, and, almost all the way to the cemetery where absolution was to take place in the chapel, the last carriage was separated from the others, as if it weren't a part of the same funeral.

Graux, Loursat, Monde and Bouvet. Each, after his different fashion, has made his way through the clashing rocks of Sim's Symplegades: the first has out-faced his infatuation; the second, by overcoming his seclusion and selfishness, has discovered a newly awakened interest in the world of human beings—however transitory that interest may prove, for one has a sneaking feeling that Loursat will renege and retreat back behind his green baize door, to his library and his musty bottles. M. Monde, through a combination of resolve and good luck—his disappearance, his meeting with Julie and the loss of his money—has shed his fears and uncertainties. And just as M. Monde cannot help recalling ruefully that his father, that unfeeling scoundrel and waster, was beloved and cossetted by all around him, so the life of the mysterious and unrepentant M. Bouvet has only served to prove once more (all too literally, as a Bertillon fingerprint of 1897 remains to show) that a certain kind of human-being can get away with murder.

Chapter 7

A PERSONAL CANON

EVERY reader of Simenon has his own list of preferences, not so much in terms of merit as of personal choice; the two categories do, of course, overlap, though not as often in the case of Simenon as in those of more homogeneous and less Protean writers. For example, Miss Brophy, as we have seen, greatly favours *Le Train*, which I personally find not at all out of the ordinary, while other deeply-read admirers make large claims for *Les Anneaux de Bicêtre*, to my mind a rather lifeless book. Sir Herbert Read, one of the earliest and most judicious champions of Simenon's work in this country, who, as his original English publisher, did so much to promote him in translation, has likewise left an interesting record of his own preferences. In this chapter I have made an attempt to set out my own canon—excluding the Maigret series and the later novels, which I have deliberately set apart from the rest, believing that in *Le Petit Saint* (1965) Simenon did achieve an imaginative breakthrough which has given a new turn to his fiction. In this chapter, therefore, I can only strike an impressionistic and personal note.

In *Lettre à mon Juge* (1947) Charles Alavoine, a middle-aged doctor from the Vendée, sets out to explain how he came to strangle his mistress. In a long letter to the examining magistrate, written from prison after he has been sentenced, he tells the story of his life. He is writing it because 'I should like one man, just one, to understand me. And I would like that man to be you'. (Remembering the large and unsympathetic part that M. Ernest Coméliau, to whom the letter is addressed, plays in the Maigret saga, the reader may be permitted to raise an eyebrow!)

This is perhaps the most perfectly constructed of all Simenon's novels. It has an interior, passionate logic of its own, each act of the drama leading up to the cumulative tragedy being beautifully proportioned and set out. The book imposes the same sense of classic inevitability as the reader discovers (dare I say it?) in the story of Emma Bovary herself. Certainly, in spite of its ending and the use of the first person, it is the only one of Simenon's books that you could call, in the remotest sense, Flaubertian.

Alavoine begins by describing the feeling of unreality he experienced in the courtroom—the glib questions and phrases, all mouthed in total indifference to the truth of life as it really happens. (As poor Mlle. Blanche murmurs, when questioned about her relationship with M. Bouvet: 'It wasn't like that.') He describes his own mother's appearance as a witness—her bewilderment, her shame, 'not ashamed of me, as the reporters wrote, but ashamed of being the target of all those eyes, ashamed at disturbing such important persons, she who had always felt herself of so little account':

> Poor Mama. She was dressed in black. For over thirty years she has worn nothing but black from head to foot, like most of our peasant women at home. Knowing her as I do, she must have worried about what she should wear, must have asked my wife's advice. I'd be willing to swear that she repeated at least a dozen times: 'I am so afraid of disgracing him!'
> It was certainly my wife who suggested the thin lace collar, so that her clothes would look less like mourning, so that she would not seem to be trying to play on the jury's sympathy.

He describes his childhood in the Vendée and his supposedly jovial alcoholic father, the once prosperous farmer, always doing the fairs, having the girls, shooting everything in sight and selling a piece of land every season ('just a splinter, as we say'), eventually killing himself. He tells of his beginnings as a country doctor, his young wife's death in pregnancy, and his removal to a better practice with his mother keeping house for him. Out of all this, brilliantly told, the figure of Alavoine, the peasant's son turned first-generation professional man, emerges clearly—awkward, conformist, strongly-sexed without ever having known anything more than physical passion. The whole narrative prepares us for the arrival of Armande, the provincially fashionable widow, dominant, predatory, condescendingly ironic towards the old mother at the Alavoines' disastrous evening party (a cruelly Flaubertian episode, this). Armande, cat-like, inserts herself into the Alavoine household, nurses his child through diphtheria, marries the doctor, pushes his mother pitilessly up-stage and begins improving and quietly imposing her will on the pair of them:

> Have you ever dreamed that you had married your schoolmistress? Well, your Honour, that is what happened to me. For ten years my mother and I, both of us, lived at school, waiting to be given a good mark, in fear of receiving a bad one . . .
> Armande, little by little, without knowing it herself, took on for me the character of Destiny. And, in revolt against that Destiny, I revolted against her . . .
> What of it! I felt the need of deceiving Armande, of deceiving my Destiny as sordidly as possible, and I chose a big blonde with a vulgar smile and a gold tooth in the front of her mouth.

After ten years of marriage, Alavoine's real tragic Destiny arrives. One evening, away from home, he meets a young girl at a railway station. In fact, it is Martine with her two suitcases and her little hat perched over one eye, in her chic tailored suit 'much too light for the season', thin, very dark, with looks like a cover girl, who picks Alavoine up. She drags him, irritated but resigned, round the bars and dance halls of the town, drinking, cutting capers, showing off, demanding to be noticed at all costs:

> 'Barman, a martini, please . . .'
> I'd much rather not talk about her as I saw her that evening, your Honour, but then you wouldn't understand, and my letter would be useless. It is difficult, I assure you, especially now.
> Isn't it true, Martine, that it is difficult?
> Because, you see, she was such a banal little thing. She was already perched on one of the stools, and one felt that she was at home there, that it was an old habit, that together with the more or less luxurious setting it formed a part of her conception of life . . .
> Martine wanted to dance and I danced with her. That was when I noticed the nape of her neck, very close and very white, with skin so fine that the blue veins showed, and little tendrils of wet hair.
> Why did her neck move me? It was, in a way, the first human thing I discovered about her . . .
> The miracle is that I met her, that double tardiness which brought us face to face. The miracle is, above all else, that I . . . Charles Alavoine, in the course of a night when I was drunk, when she too was drunk, and during which we had dragged our disgust through all the sordid rain-drenched streets of Nantes, suddenly understood.

Thus Alavoine's fatally obsessive love of Martine is born—for the real Martine, the frightened child of circumstance that lies behind the would-be slut. 'But cannot you understand that I delivered her,' he cries to the judge, 'it was not she whom I killed, it was the Other.' He introduces Martine to his home, employs her in his surgery and, when their life of lying and hiding becomes unbearable, leaves his wife and family and makes a new existence for the pair of them in Paris. He takes a working-class practice, they rent a doll's house apartment. Their idyll would appear to be complete. Yet by the very logic of their passion, their shared knowledge that Martine can never shed her second-self and that 'in spite of anything she could do, in spite of her love, her humble love . . . she was at the same time the other', Alavoine and Martine both know that death can be the only real consummation of their life together. And so, in the very act of strangling her,

> . . . I felt that she was encouraging me, that she wished it, that she had always foreseen this moment, *that it was the only way out.*
> I had to kill the Other, once and for all, so that my Martine could live at last . . .
> I am not mad. I am just a man, a man like other men, but a man who has loved, who knows what love is.
> I shall live in her, with her, for her, as long as I possibly can, and if I imposed upon myself this waiting, if I inflicted on myself that sort of circus which was called a trial, it was so that she, no matter what the cost, may continue to live in someone . . .
> We went as far as it was possible to go. We did all we possibly could.
> We wanted the totality of love.

A most un-Flaubertian conclusion, the reader may feel—pure nineteenth-century hysteria, the act of a Zola primitive or the ravings of a Léon Bloy, rather than a natural description of the human passions. Yet one can read stranger *faits divers* than this in any of the world's newspapers. Given Charles Alavoine's background, his second marriage and his obsession, the story is not only tragic and haunting but strangely credible. Besides, the idea that each man kills the thing he loves is a well-rooted one. It can always find its collateral in experience.

If *Lettre à mon Juge* is the most perfectly constructed, *La Neige*

était sale (1948) may be said to be the most sombre and powerful
of Simenon's novels. It is also the most mysterious and inexplicable—for two reasons, the one technical and the other metaphysical.
Leaving these aside for a moment, let us briefly summarize the
plot. The setting, though it is imprecisely indicated, may be said
to be a town in some Central European state under totalitarian
occupation. Simenon's imprecision is deliberate and cunning
here, since in this way he manages to obtain the maximum
dramatic effect. His army of occupation—the bullying Gestapo-
like officer who beats Frank up at headquarters, the General who
collects period watches of porcelain, the Oberleutnant-patrol
atmosphere that pervades the town—all this suggests Nazi
domination. On the other hand, the prison and interrogation
centre to which Frank is despatched is unmistakably a Soviet-
inspired institution, while the villages outside the town with their
green, pink and blue houses, 'with life-size angels painted on the
gable end . . . almost all of them with a little niche holding a
china figure of the Virgin', inevitably suggest Austrian baroque.

Amid this drab and subjugated community, its half-starved
tenement dwellers shivering with the cold, certain well-heeled
black market and collaborationist zones of food and warmth
shine out. Such a one is the Friedmaier household. Lotte
Friedmaier, fortyish, an ex-prostitute, runs a select knocking-shop
for officers under the guise of a manicure salon. No scarcities in
her *ménage*—four stoves are going full blast and the larder holds
unlimited supplies of eatables. Her son Frank, aged nineteen,
is a youth of parts: pimp, procurer for his mother (whom he
coldly detests) and go-between in all kinds of shady deals in
collusion with his pal, Big Fred Kromer. Kromer, with his gross
physique, his bulging eyes, his wet cigar and his sexual bravura,
is the senior partner.

Across the corridor from the Friedmaiers are the Holsts, father
and daughter, he a one-time art critic and now a tram driver,
she a shy sixteen-year-old who earns a pittance by painting china.
Holst, a quietly-spoken, well-educated pauper, is rumoured to be
in the Resistance.

Lying in bed, listening to Bertha, his mother's young tart and
slavey, make the coffee, Frank finds himself thinking about the

Holsts. Last night, to prove himself, he killed a man—the fat
N.C.O. they call The Eunuch—sliding Kromer's long Swedish
knife through his ribs. He is certain that Holst, who was passing,
saw him do it. But Holst remains silent on the matter. Later, the
young violinist upstairs is arrested for Frank's crime and taken
away. Little by little, Frank reflects, the young man's old mother
will go to pieces:

> They would find her in her bedroom, dry as a mummy, dead the
> last eight or ten days.
> He felt no pity. Not for anybody. Not even for himself. He neither
> asked pity, nor would he accept it, and that was why he was so
> irritated with Lotte; she gazed fondly after him, her eyes full of
> anxiety and tenderness.
> What he would find really interesting would be a talk with Holst
> some time, a good long talk, just the two of them together. This
> desire had long been working in him, even before he was yet
> aware of it.
> Why Holst? He had no idea. Perhaps he never would know.
> He refused to think that it might be because he had never had a
> father.

As a substitute for Holst, Frank makes his daughter, the gentle
Sissy, fall in love with him. Meanwhile there is the General,
Kromer's General, lusting for rare watches and prepared to pay
anything to gratify his mania. Frank knows where to get watches
and he obtains them, but in doing so he kills the dead watchmaker's
sister, an old woman who has been kind to him throughout his
childhood. This second killing is quite different from the first
since 'oddly enough, it now seemed to him that he had just
accomplished an inevitable act, an act of whose necessity he had
long had a presentiment'. From this point on Frank's whole
stature changes. Hitherto he has seemed little more than a cool-
nerved, ruthless young gangster—a pale approximation to the
Pinkie of *Brighton Rock* with sex, drink, tobacco and two years
on his age added and without the theological ballast. Now, 'at
bottom they were all somewhat in fear of him, because he had
set his course for the ultimate limit'.

The 'ultimate limit' takes the form of persuading Sissy to sleep
with him and then, in the darkened bedroom and by skilful stage-
management, ensuring that she be raped by Kromer, whose

sexual boastings have proved false and whose reputation as a deflowerer of virgins has been sadly tarnished:

> He must be got to take another drink, otherwise he would falter. And he must not falter at any price. Frank had worked out the whole plan like a piece of clockwork, with the meticulous care of a child.
>
> Some things cannot be explained, and it is useless trying to make anyone else understand: this thing just had to happen. After that he could rest easy . . .
>
> To think that only ten days before he had looked on Kromer as an older man, as a man much stronger than himself, as—in short— a man, while he had regarded himself as nothing but a boy!

The plot misfires, all too horribly, and Sissy, screaming Frank's name, runs from the house into the snow. (This is one of the cruellest glimpses of the 'accepted hells beneath' that Simenon's imagination has ever conceived.) As for Frank, he

> . . . had done what he wanted. He had seen what was on the other side.
>
> He had not seen what he expected to see. No matter! . . .
>
> Would nobody realize that he had reached the other side of the turning, that he had nothing in common with any of them any more?

Sissy is brought home by her father, the scandal is hushed up, things quieten down. 'You can tell Christmas is coming,' says Lotte, *'the faces are beginning to change'*—meaning that the civil and military staffs of the occupying power are changing. 'Some went home to their own country, and others came from there, new men with different names and unknown characters.' Frank forces the pace, flinging his prize money about everywhere, getting drunk, picking quarrels, flaunting the coveted green identity card which was part of his bargain with the General:

> For he wanted fate to take notice of him. He had done everything possible to force it to do so, and he continued to challenge it from morning to night. The day before he had said to Kromer with studied negligence:
>
> 'Ask your general, will you, what he'd like, apart from watches.' . . .
>
> Fate was lying in wait for him somewhere. But where? Instead of waiting for fate to reveal itself at its appointed time, Frank ran after it, casting about everywhere in his search . . .
>
> And it was in the morning, when he had yet another hangover, that it happened. He had searched for fate in every corner, and fate was in none of the places where he had hunted.

For Lotte's new brooms have been at work. One morning, quite suddenly, Frank is led away to a prison outside the town and to endless interrogation at the hands of a Kafka-like being whom he thinks of as 'the old gentleman'. And so he begins his long and sleepless atonement—what M. de Fallois, in his study of Simenon, speaks of approvingly as his *'expiation'*. It is an expiation which, though a wonderfully sustained piece of writing, goes on for far too long—for roughly one-quarter the length of the book almost as though the writer were determined that his reader should share in Frank's repentance (perhaps that is the effect that he intended). This is the inexplicable element about the book mentioned earlier. Far from hastening and foreshortening the ending, as he so often does in his fiction, Simenon, in this instance, has paradoxically chosen to drag out the last act of his tragedy. On second thoughts, there may be good reason for this. The climax, when it comes, is magnificent, yet it implies such a metamorphosis of feeling in Frank himself as could only be justified after this manner.

The interrogation continues. For Frank, stalling 'the old gentleman' has long become his only reason for existence. He knows his grey-haired inquisitor will win in the end but each day gained and notched up in his classroom cell has somehow become a victory (this idea of the prison having previously been a school is part of the weird Kafkaesque atmosphere in which this last section of the novel is couched). His mother visits him—and is rejected outright. But during their interview, she asks him what he'd like her to bring him next time:

> He said, almost inaudibly, conscious of what the words meant for him, but for him alone:
> 'Could I see Holst?'

Frank trades the information he has withheld for so long and permission is granted. At last he has his confrontation with the man whose daughter he has betrayed, the man who most of all he has wished to question. And Holst gives his explanation of why for him 'everything matters equally'. Solemnly, 'in a voice at once grave and toneless which recalled certain ceremonies of Holy Week', he recites the facts of his son's suicide:

Frank would have liked to say something to him. There was one thing in particular he would have liked to tell him, but which meant nothing, which might be taken amiss; he would have liked to be Holst's son, he would like to be Holst's son. It would make him so happy—and ease him of such a burden—if he could say the one word:

'Father!'

Sissy had the right to do that—Sissy, whose eyes never left him. He could not tell . . . whether she was thinner or paler. That didn't count. She had come. It was she who had wished to come, and Holst had agreed. Holst took her by the hand, and brought her to Frank.

'There,' he concluded. 'It's a tough job to be a human being.' . . . He turned towards the window, so that they might look at each other, just the two of them.

There were no rings. There was no key. Neither were there any prayers, but Holst's words took their place.

Sissy was there. Holst was there . . .

She had come. She was there. She was in him. She was his. Holst had blessed them.

Through what aberration, or unheard-of generosity, did fate, after a gift such as so few men are allowed, now grant Frank another? Instead of questioning him, as in all likelihood should have happened, the old gentleman got up, put on his hat and coat—a thing that had never occurred before—and Frank was taken back to his room.

There, in the realization that 'it did not matter how long a thing lasted. What did matter was that it should exist', Frank waits for the firing squad.

Alavoine kills Martine (and takes his own life in the prison infirmary) as a surety that 'the totality' of their love will be realized and perpetuated. Frank goes to his death knowing that 'although there would be no window that opened, no washing out to dry, no cradle', 'this was his own marriage! It was his honeymoon, it was his life which he must live in one close packed instant, near the old gentleman fumbling among his scraps of paper'. Both embrace death as the sublime and possibly the only safe way of witnessing to a human absolute, a state of ecstasy and fulfilment. In this sense they are as much devotees of Saint-Genet as major characters of Simenon's imagination. For the hero, Genet tells us,

 . . . tragedy is a joyous moment . . . The hero cannot sulk at a heroic death. He is a hero only because of that death. It is the condition so bitterly sought by creatures without glory; itself is glory; it is (this death and the accumulation of the apparent misfortunes leading to it) the crowning of a predisposed life . . .

Frank is Simenon's Stavrogin, his dark prince. If he is not 'the source of the chaos that streams through the characters', it certainly can be said that he 'possesses them but is not himself possessed'.[1] Dieudonné Ferchaux and Michel Maudet, the twin heroes of *L'Aîné des Ferchaux* (1945), form a weird variation on the relationship between Vautrin and Lucien de Rubempré, as related in the second part of Balzac's *Les Illusions Perdues*. Ferchaux, the shark millionaire of the French Congo on the run for the murders he committed years ago in Africa, and Maudet, the poor boy from the provinces burning with ambition, make perfect foils for the best of all Simenon's pure melodramas.

In a prologue of less than ten pages, Simenon places the situation of the two Ferchaux brothers who, coming penniless to Africa in the Nineties, carved a commercial empire out of ebony and coconut and rubber. Emile, the youngest, returned to Paris to direct the enterprise and fulfil the obvious ambitions—marrying a Prefect's daughter, buying a château, entertaining the Cabinet, etc. Dieudonné stayed on, preferring to become an evil legend, living rough, chugging up the river in his motorboat, losing a leg through gangrene, enjoying the favours of his native wives or those of his white employees, hurling sticks of dynamite at his bearers when they threatened to abandon him. Year by year the legend had grown blacker. Now, through the zeal of a slighted petty official whom the Shark, out of pride, has refused to conciliate, a national scandal has broken. There have been ministerial resignations, newspaper editorials, speeches in the Chamber—the whole French establishment is in the throes of a new Panama. Meanwhile, the elder Ferchaux has returned quietly to France and gone to ground without trace. It is at this point that Michel Maudet, aged twenty, brash, impulsive, temperamental, avid for life and adventure, being on his beam ends in Paris and hearing that a certain M. Dieudonné requires a secretary, a post offering exciting prospects, impulsively dashes to

[1] See Irving Howe's 'Dostoevsky and the Politics of Salvation' (*Politics and the Novel*), quoted by George Steiner in *Tolstoy or Dostoevsky*.

Caen, dragging his protesting young wife with him. The novel proper begins appropriately on the night train with the impetuous Maudet thrusting the terrified Lina into a first-class compartment in defiance of the ticket collector.

Like all the best melodramas, the plot of *L'Aîné des Ferchaux* is too elaborate, and too good, to summarize. How Maudet is accepted as Ferchaux's secretary and inducted into the strange set-up at La Guillerie, how he and Lina join the old Shark in his secret flight from Caen to Dunkirk and how, the first stage of their strange relationship accomplished, Michel deserts Lina and sails with his master (master for how long?) to South America—all this, with what befalls the pair in Panama and the grim *dénouement* that puts an end to their partnership, should be read for the story itself. At that level alone it remains the pick of Simenonian 'entertainments'.

There is, however, much more to the book than that. How much more seems at first to depend on whether we see the crux of the novel as lying in the relationship between the two men or in the developing character of Maudet himself. The stages in Maudet's attitude towards his employer are clearly marked. From awe and anxious subservience ('All I ask is for you to give me a chance') to pride at being the great man's confidant and being involved in big events ('He was up to his neck in it. He was playing an active part in the drama') to the point where Ferchaux, till now so full of fight, viciously counter-attacking his enemies through his newspaper revelations, first shows signs of fear—not so much fear of arrest and imprisonment as fear of being alone. As Michel, having walked out on Lina, comes aboard, Ferchaux stares intensely 'at the young man who had consented to throw in his lot with him':

> A glow of triumph came into his eyes, but it was immediately extinguished by the smile that hovered on Michel's thin lips, a smile that no one had ever seen there before.
> It was no longer the tense, over-wrought boy of the last few weeks; it was another person who stood there, someone colder and made of harder stuff. His gaze wandered, taking in his surroundings, resting for a moment on the picture of a naked girl at the head of the bunk. His upper lip curled slightly as though promising this new person that all his appetites would be gratified.

Everything that we have deduced about Michel from the beginning, everything Lina dimly divined when he pulled her into the railway carriage, is now made plain: 'At that moment he seemed to her like some young animal that, by dint of guile and perseverance, had at last won its way into its proper element.'

After that Panama, with Ferchaux ill and emaciated, his fire extinguished, surrounded by medicine bottles, dictating his memoirs and determined to leave nothing out ('It was since he had started on his memoirs that he had become so scared of death'). Maudet, straining at the leash, grows more exasperated and unfeeling as the old man grows more and more demanding. 'Three years he had been boxed up with him. And that was enough. More than enough . . . If Michel had been asked what he considered the ugliest thing in the world, he would without hesitation have answered: An old man's hairy chest.'

From here it is only a few pages to the moment of ugliest truth. Leaning across his bar, Jeff, the huge ex-convict (he still shaves his head out of pride), speaks musingly to Michel:

> 'During westerly gales, bodies were thrown up on the beach. Three in two months. They weren't exactly Europeans, but native people with more or less white skins. The darkest was a pale coffee colour. All three were alike in one respect: they were all old and their heads were missing.'
>
> Michel was drinking in every word.
>
> 'You see, white heads sell better than the coloured ones,' said Jeff, as though that explained everything. 'Besides, old heads are in great demand because they have more expression. They dry quicker, too.'

We take leave of Michel, now known as Captain Phillips, in Singapore:

> Young, slim and sunburnt, he went in for every sport and was ready for any game. He kept polo ponies, danced to perfection, and took his spirits neat.
>
> In spite of his youth, a few grey hairs showed at his temples, and his smile was haunted by an unfathomable irony. In his light blue eyes there was a fixity which contrasted with his conviviality.
>
> He had a way of saying jocularly—at least his friends always took it as a joke: 'I'm quite an old man, you know . . .'
>
> And when they all protested, it gave him a peculiar satisfaction to be the only one to know that it was true.

Homosexuality holds a minimal interest for Simenon and plays little or no part in his fiction. It is one of the few aspects of human nature with which he appears to be relatively unfamiliar (though lesbians are likewise at a discount). In the hundred or so novels of his that I have read I cannot think of more than twenty characters who were homosexually inclined and all of them are quite marginal figures or walk-on parts (with the possible exception of the villain of *Maigret chez le Ministre,* where the characteristic is little more than hinted at). It is not surprising, therefore, that while the reader may scent a rough literary parallel between Ferchaux and Maudet and Vautrin and Rubempré, Michel explicitly disclaims a 'vicious' side to his relationship with the old man when Lina jealously taxes him with it. Maudet does resemble Rubempré in that his is not, when all is said, a genuine but, rather, a spurious ambition: both are creatures of appetite and all they both want is luxury and an easy life. Lina, after Ferchaux has conquered her by his unaccustomed courtesy and attentions (much to Maudet's chagrin and wounded amour-propre) assures her husband that 'You remind him of himself, of his youth, of the boy he once was. Sometimes he positively winces at some word, a gesture of yours. He seems surprised and troubled . . .' In copying his master's ruthlessness—and justifying it by Ferchaux's own tale of violence in the jungle—the *chela* proves himself the most faithful of disciples!

At a second reading, *Le Voyageur de la Toussaint* (1941) seems a slighter work than one had first imagined—certainly far slighter than the sombre and perhaps intentionally cumbrous *Le Testament Donadieu* (1937), that grim indictment of the provincial haute-bourgeoisie. La Rochelle has a special place in Simenon's affections—though, judging by *Le Testament,* one would scarcely imagine so. With the exception of Martine Dargens, *née* Donadieu, and her husband's father, Frédéric, that humane man of pleasure, there is scarcely a character in the large cast that the author has assembled who is neither vicious, worthless, wooden, nor neurotic. The book is oppressive and doom-laden to a general degree that is rare in Simenon, for whom the individual tragedy is normally the rub. Here the requiem for Martine and Philippe becomes a collective *Dies Irae* for the whole Donadieu tribe and, by extension, for the French bourgeoisie of the Nineteen-Thirties. In Sartre's terms, Simenon might legitimately claim to have taken hold of his own 'historical patch of time' in this book—that is, if he cared to do so, which is doubtful. It is ironically significant that the only overt political act in the novel is sparked off by private emotions of an old-fashioned and entirely non-political order, i.e. when Baillet, the engine-driver, enraged at his daughter's seduction by her employer, Michel Donadieu, brandishes his bright new Communist Party card in Odette's face.

Le Voyageur, on the other hand, though it is also set in La Rochelle and deals with much the same milieu, is couched in an entirely different vein of feeling. You could almost call it a grim-gay pantomime of provincial life, a Jack the Giant Killer fantasy which turns suddenly, in the epilogue, into harlequinade. It begins strikingly enough on All Souls' Eve with nineteen-year-old Gilles Mauvoisin stealthily arriving by water in the city he has never known but which his dead parents' memories have bequeathed him. Having eloped from La Rochelle years ago, Gilles' father and mother have led a wandering life in the music-halls, café-concerts and circuses of Europe, he as violinist and conjurer, she as his patron and assistant. Now suddenly they have both died while performing at Trondjhem and Gilles, who has known nothing but the backstage world of clowns and dressing-rooms, cues and theatrical digs and beginners' overtures all his life, must suddenly enter upon his strange bourgeois inheritance. His innocent and headlong plunge from the tinsel make-believe world of wet-white to the sinister wet paint of provincial intrigue and counter-plot and his eventual re-emergence, is the theme of this most readable, gamey and fundamentally unserious of Simenon's fictions—a novel in which Sim, the demiurge, has surely been given more than his head.

I say unserious, not only in contradistinction to *Le Testament Donadieu* but because the whole plot, sub-plot, machinery and characterization of the book is nothing more than good theatre of the best boulevard vintage. Simenon himself is allowed to do little more than make sentimental noises:

Two people had come together long ago and fled this town to wander from place to place and end up in a little Norwegian port. And a little while ago their son had stood under a stone-pine pressing a girl to his breast, gazing into her eyes, close to his. And he had asked her to become one with him for ever.

His grip tightened on Colette's shoulder, yet he hardly knew whether it was hers or Alice's, or even his mother's. It was the shoulders of a woman, the woman of all time, who walks by the side of a man into the darkness of the unknown . . . and who suffers . . .

All the rest is drawn from Sim's almanack of fates and answers. The sinister 'Syndicate' of business and professional men who control the city with their legalized Mafia-hand—the Senator, the big shipowner, the timber king, the Prosecutor General, the lawyer, and Gilles' macabre Aunt Gérardine; Uncle Octave, who controlled them in life and who hag-rides them from the grave through the contents of his safe with its mysterious five-letter combination—all this is first-class derring-do. As 'the heir of a man whom everybody feared', and to discover who poisoned him, Gilles is forced to retrace the daily round made by his uncle, Stalin of the bus companies, the fish market, the newspapers and the local bank:

'What did he come here for?' asked Gilles, who was beginning to feel uncomfortable under so many staring eyes.

'Just to see! . . . And there certainly wasn't much that escaped his eye. He made a mental note of the day's prices and from the number of lots he had a very shrewd idea of the day's catch . . . If anyone tried to do him down he'd see through it at once.' . . .

And Gilles had the feeling he was beginning to understand. Those men at work were aware only of appearances, the slippery translucent blocks of ice, the slow rumbling of their horse-drawn van over the uneven cobbles. They lived on the surface of a world at the centre of which was Octave Mauvoisin. Whatever form activity might take, he was so to speak the pivot of it. If Ouvrard was telephoning to a stockbroker in Paris, it would be because of a note scrawled in red pencil . . .

When the well-groomed Edgard Plantel sat down at his mahogany desk he looked a very imposing figure. But that too was a façade, for behind him, looking over his shoulder, was the shadow of Octave Mauvoisin . . .

Goods trucks were shunted into sidings . . . Trawlers put to sea and returned with their fish-holds full . . . Hundreds of men and women went to work in the mornings and hurried home at night

with an eye on the clock . . . Ships brought cargoes from Bergen or
Liverpool . . .

> . . . The port was bathed in sunshine. The busy crowd round him
was colourful and gay. Its laughter rang in his ears. But through it
stalked Octave Mauvoisin, a stocky ghost with heavy tread, casting
a deathly shadow over all.
> He would have liked to brush away that image, to take a deep
breath and get back into the land of the living.

Alas, the 'land of the living' is not nearly so entertaining as the
ogreish mock-up of La Rochelle. *Le Voyageur de la Toussaint* is
one of those prize good-bad books of which Orwell wrote with
such affection. One only wishes that it were twice as long as it is.

Finally, *Le Grand Bob* (1954)—my own favourite among all
Simenon's works of fiction. Less than two hundred pages in
length, it sums up and concentrates his many-sided genius in a
way that is limpid yet ambiguous, a microcosm of his whole
achievement. Like all his best work, the book can be read at
several levels—as the story of a mysterious death by drowning
and what lay behind it, as a study in character, as a view of life
seen from the standpoint of the eternal onlooker. In this respect
it could be described as a study of *désinvolture*, a comment on
the beginning of two of La Rochefoucauld's maxims, namely
that 'There are people whose defects become them' and that
'We make a mistake if we believe that only the violent passions
like ambition and love can subdue the others. Laziness, for all
her languor, is nevertheless often mistress'. Lastly, the book
could simply be described as a love story in which love is founded
on pity. Deceptively slight, it contains some of Simenon's most
profound comments upon life and human beings. The story
itself is told by Bob's friend, Charles Coindreau, a Parisian doctor
in general practice.

At the age of about fifty, Bob Durandand is the kind of man
whom his friends consider an open and companionable enigma.
His wife Lulu runs a hat shop, he himself does—what exactly?
Certainly not very much, beyond playing *belote*, telling droll
stories and frequenting the small bars in his section of Montmartre.

During the fourteen or so years that Coindreau has known him, Durandand has held some twenty different jobs. For example, he has been publicity agent for a magazine, he has represented a shoe firm; he has generally left these positions of his own accord, though not always, since he has never seemed able to take the task of earning his living at all seriously. Tall, loose-limbed, easy-going, mischievous, full of genial malice, he is, as his staider friends would say, one of nature's bohemians, a boulevardier who prefers the snug warmth of his own district to the café society of the grand boulevards. He is a clown, a natural farceur of the first order. In their flat behind the shop in the Rue Lamarck Bob and Lulu keep open house. 'At any hour one was certain to find company . . . Bob's first remark was invariably *"Un coup de blanc?"* . . . In a sense his home was neutral ground, almost like a café but a café where everyone was free to speak and act in his own fashion, certain that nothing he said or did could ever shock the company.' Bob's favourite expression, *'Crevant!'*[1] sums up his public reaction to life generally.

Each week-end Bob and Lulu foregather with friends at a fishermen's inn on the Seine—a cheerful, familiar place, more like a country club than an inn, where the guests are mostly *habitués*, knowing and enjoying one another's company though sharply divided into two amicable factions. There are the anglers and the non-anglers, the intent, passionate fraternity of fishermen who retire early and get up at 4 a.m. and the lie-abeds who stay up late drinking, playing cards and dancing to the gramophone and only emerge from their rooms around midday. Each group complains of its opposite; the early-rising anglers at the noise the others make late at night, the late risers at the way the fishermen's outboard motor engines disturb their sleep in the early morning. Previously, Le Grand Bob has been a firm non-angler. For the last two week-ends, however, he has evinced a strange desire to take up fishing. On the second Sunday morning his body is found floating in a nearby weir. Though the circumstantial evidence points to suicide, the cause of death remains unknown. It is at this point that Coindreau, who has not been

[1] Something a good deal stronger than the English 'splitting!' or the 'killing!' of girls' public-school usage; more like 'Fit to split your guts!'

at the inn that week-end, begins his own enquiries—enquiries that throw a strange new light upon Bob Durandand and on his apparent aimless and amiable existence.

Everything his friend learns about Bob's death suggests that it was not only intentional but that it was a long-planned affair, an act deliberately thought out, in no way the effect of sudden impulse or melancholia. 'Having decided to kill himself, he was concerned to do so decently. It was in character. He had run through all the forms of suicide, searching for the one that would look most like accident.' Bob's behaviour on the Saturday afternoon, the last time he slept with Adeline, his wife's employee, seems to bear this out. Usually so light-hearted in bed, he takes leave of the girl with a seriousness out of all keeping with his character. Though Adeline herself cannot explain it, Coindreau believes that he can. 'She was the last woman Bob would hold in his arms,' he reflects, 'entering the hotel bedroom, he was aware that he was about to make love for the last time.'

As Coindreau's story unfolds, Bob's whole character changes, taking on a new depth and stature. Lulu relates the story of their life together, from her first meeting with him in a café, some time in 1930, when he was an elegant young student, the son of a noted Professor of the Law Faculty, and she a poor girl with no background, half-heartedly sleeping around on the Left Bank in hopes of the real love affair that never materialized. They dine, he gets drunk and they spend the night together; the following morning he is due to take his law exam. When the time comes, despite Lulu's entreaties, he fails to present himself for the examination. Again a deliberate choice, for it turns out Bob has never wished to be a lawyer. As though recognizing his mission in life, he takes Lulu—pathetic, trusting, devoted Lulu—under his protection. They live together for years and eventually get married. 'When Bob adopted Lulu,' Coindreau tells himself,

> . . . he accepted entire responsibility for her. He never made great speeches to her. He never even spoke of love. He took her by the hand like a child, like the small girl that she was and she, surprised at first that a great boy like this should stoop towards her, had confidence in him and so in life itself.
>
> I found myself envying the pair of them. I began to understand

the atmosphere of serene gaiety that surrounded them. They denied all importance to the inessential, and that was why I and those like me went so often to the studio in the Rue Lamarck, and felt so heartened there.

Among the mourners at Bob's funeral, Coindreau has caught a glimpse of the dead man's sister, Mme. Pétrel, an elegant distinguished-looking woman, married to a well-known barrister, and her son, Jean-Paul. The latter's appearance and bearing impress Coindreau as giving an idea of what Bob Durandand must have looked like as a young man and it comes as no surprise to learn that Jean-Paul worshipped his uncle. Later, he meets the Pétrels at a dinner-party. During a long conversation with Mme. Pétrel after the meal, a great deal about the mystery of Durandand's character and background is explained. In discussing Hector Loursat, we noted Simenon's sneaking admiration of the *noblesse de robe* tradition. Germaine Pétrel, the sympathetic patrician, is a visible embodiment of the type. With a warm clarity, choosing her words carefully and giving everyone their due, she sets out the facts of her brother's youth and upbringing:

> She had no need to improvise. It was clear that she had thought about these matters for a long time and I suspected, knowing through Saucier [their host] that I would speak of her brother, she had prepared certain replies to my questions, not in order to shine in conversation or set the family in a good light but rather from careful concern to relate the exact truth. She hesitated over each phrase, returning sometimes to correct a detail, to add a nuance . . .

It is in this way that Coindreau learns how, at seventeen, Bob Durandand's secret ambition was to be a priest in the Sahara. 'He had a great map of North Africa in his room, a photograph of Père de Foucauld which he had found heaven knows where and an ebony crucifix.' Later, his ambitions changed and he took a job as an unskilled worker at the Citroën plant among the Arabs from the *zones*. Learning all this for the first time, Coindreau reflects that the curve of Durandand's life was not after all surprising. From dreaming of a priest's life in Africa to working humbly in a factory, he moved to a middle position—an idler's existence among the *bistros* of Montmartre. 'It was rather as if Bob, having aimed too high and then too low in life, had at length come to rest in a state of joyous mediocrity':

> Certainly he was a *raté*, as I've heard many declare since his death, but he was a lucid and conscious *raté*, one who had deliberately chosen this condition. In my eyes his life took on a certain grandeur.
> Having wished to be a saint in the desert and then a humble worker, he had finished, quite simply, as he had told his sister, by making one person happy.

It remains for Germaine's husband, the dry, analytical and somewhat unsympathetic lawyer, to clinch the matter in Bob's own words:

> 'Once when my wife asked him if he was happy, he replied that he wouldn't have changed his life for anyone.
> 'I believe they spoke that day of the visit Robert paid his father at Christmas, the year he abandoned his studies so abruptly . . .
> 'She asked him: "You've no regrets?"
> 'After a moment's thought, he replied: "In any case, I've made one person happy and I'll continue doing so."
> 'Then he laughed, mocking himself as always, and adding: "In fact, if each of us charged ourselves with the happiness of someone else, *le monde entier serait heureux.*" '

The story of Bob and Lulu would appear to be expressed in the simplest of formulas: he for life only (*'Crevant!'*), she for life in him. The reason for his carefully camouflaged suicide is explained, as the reader will perhaps have guessed, by the simple fact of cancer.

Le Grand Bob is a haunting book, not only in terms of its hero himself, but in the questions that his life necessarily raises; also, for the light that he and Lulu together throw on the characters surrounding them. Their essential happiness acts as a touchstone for the measurement of others' complicated designs for living and disquietingly completes the first of the Rochefoucauld maxims already quoted—namely, that if 'there are people whose defects become them', there are 'others who are ill served by their good qualities'. Coindreau's wife Madeleine, as the doctor sadly realizes in the event, is one of these, but she is by no means the only one. Setting aside the salutary wisdom implied by Maigret, *Le Grand Bob* is the greatest of Simenon's lay sermons of insouciance and love.

Chapter 8

THE MENDER OF DESTINIES

It may be odd but this feeling had its roots in his dreams as a child, as an adolescent. Although the death of his father had interrupted his medical studies after their second year, he had never really intended to become a proper doctor, to care for the sick.

To tell the truth, the profession he had always wanted to practise did not exist. Even when quite young, he had always felt that lots of people in his village were not in their right niche, were treading paths which were not theirs, solely because they were not aware.

And he used to imagine a very intelligent man, above all a very understanding man, doctor and priest at once, as it were, a man who would at first glance understand the destinies of others.

People would have come to consult this man, just as they consulted a doctor. In a manner of speaking he would have been a repairer of destinies. Not only because he was intelligent. Maybe he wouldn't have needed to be exceptionally intelligent? But because he was able to live the lives of every sort of man, to put himself inside everybody's mind.

Maigret had never mentioned this to anybody; he didn't dare think about it too much, or he would have started laughing at himself. Unable to finish his medical studies, he had entered the police force, almost by accident. Was it really such an accident?

And are not policemen actually repairers of destinies sometimes?

The chronicles of Maigret are fortunately so well known that it is unnecessary to examine his case-book in detail or even to summarize any of his more famous adventures. (Since Simenon's later fiction is mostly concerned with placing and developing a situation rather than telling a story, reader and writer can be excused any further analysis of plot.) The pipe, the heavy over-coat, the anachronistic bowler, repudiated by Maigret himself, the office in the Quai des Orfèvres with its view of the Seine and its old-fashioned black stove, the glass-fronted waiting room, the trays of beer and sandwiches sent in from the Brasserie Dauphine across the way—all these stage properties have likewise passed into legend. In this chapter I shall be concerned only to hazard my own conception of the Chief-Inspector, based, not on the whole corpus of some seventy titles in which he figures or even on the forty-odd that I have read, but on the dozen or so particular volumes on which his character and personality seem most definitely stamped and in which he is quintessentially himself.

Strictly and unkindly speaking, one could say that there are three Maigrets—on the lines of Philip Guedalla's enumeration of the three Henry Jameses, James the First, James the Second and the Old Pretender.[1] There is certainly Maigret the First—a false or rough-hewn and uncompleted Maigret, the harsh, red-faced, suitably bowler-hatted investigator of *Le Pendu de Saint-Pholien*—just as there is, in one or two of the later volumes, something of an Old Pretender. In between—indeed, all through the series, as much in some of the earliest adventures as in his most recent—is the Maigret that we recognize and feel we know.

'A repairer of destinies.' Though the phrase is given its fullest explanation in the passage from *La Première Enquête de Maigret* quoted above, its origin derives from the tragedy of Maigret's own childhood, described in the *Mémoires*. As we know, Maigret's father was bailiff at the château of the Comte de Saint-Fiacre, in the Allier district of the Auvergne. In a neighbouring village lived a Doctor Victor Gadelle, an alcoholic who 'drank more heavily than any peasant in the neighbourhood':

> How, under these conditions, could he have been my father's friend? That remained a mystery to me. The fact remains that he often came to see him and chat with him at our home and that there was even a ritual, which consisted of taking out of the glass-fronted sideboard, as soon as he arrived, a small decanter of brandy that was kept for his exclusive use . . .
>
> He was drinking less, however. People said they never saw him tipsy now. One night he was sent for to the remotest of the farms for a confinement, and he acquitted himself with honour. On his way home he called at our house, and I remember he was very pale; I can still see my father clasping his hand with unwonted persistence as though to encourage him, as though to tell him: 'You see, things weren't so hopeless after all.'

---

[1] M. Gilbert Sigaux, in his Preface to Volume III in the collected and definitive edition of Simenon (Edition Rencontre, Lausanne, 1967), would posit four Maigrets, but this is purely a bibliophilic distinction.

For my father never gave up hope of people . . . And when my
mother was pregnant, a certain feeling which I find it hard to explain,
but which I understand, obliged him to see the thing through . . .

My mother died at seven in the morning, as day was breaking,
and when I went downstairs the first thing that caught my eye, in
spite of my emotion, was the decanter on the dining-room table . . .

I never saw Doctor Gadelle cross our threshold since that day,
but neither did I ever hear my father say one word about him.

All this causes the young Maigret to reflect—and so, un-
knowingly, prepare the way for his future vocation as a policeman:

For years, without realizing it, I tried to understand the drama of
this man at grips with a destiny that was too great for him.

And I remembered my father's attitude towards him. I wondered
whether my father had understood the same thing that I had,
whether that was why, at whatever cost to himself, he had let the
man try his luck.

From Gadelle I went on instinctively to consider the majority of
the people I had known, almost all of them simple folk with
apparently straightforward lives, who none the less had had at one
time or another to measure themselves against destiny . . .

I think that was it; I felt dimly that too many people were not in
their right places, that they were striving to play parts that were
beyond their capacities, so that the game was lost for them before
they started.

The *Mémoires* are good reading in their own right, especially
as telling the story of the young policeman's courtship of Louise
Léonard, the future Mme. Maigret, who, although she may have
begun as another of the Chief-Inspector's stage properties, has
long ago been transformed into a key character in the saga (not,
however, in her own particular adventure, *L'Amie de Madame
Maigret*, a bitty and tiresome affair). The book is also admirable
as a description of Maigret's relationship with his creator, the
blithe and cocky young man who breezes into the Inspector's
office and lectures him on the double-facedness of truth: 'At
the time of our first encounter, in the autumn, he had not been
lacking in self-confidence. Thanks to success, he was brimming
over with it now, he had enough to spare for all the timid folk
on earth.

'Was it absolutely necessary to simplify *me*?'
'To begin with, it certainly was. The public has to get used to
you, to your figure, your bearing. I've probably hit on the right

expression. For the moment you're still only a silhouette, a back, a pipe, a way of talking, of muttering.'

'Thanks!'

'The details will appear gradually, you'll see. I don't know how long it will take. Little by little you'll begin to live with a more subtle, more complex life.'

'That's reassuring.'

All this is excellent fooling—aseptic too, since by admitting all the contradictions of place, chronology and so on, Simenon has queered the pitch for any readers who might be tempted to create a fan club for Maigret on the lines of the Sherlock Holmes Society or suchlike.[1] The real value of the *Mémoires* is that they serve to establish the yardstick on which all Maigret's judgments, not only of men but of society also, are based. In that section of his fine essay on Simenon that deals specifically with Maigret ('*Epopée*'),[2] Bernard de Fallois remarks on the Chief-Inspector's apolitical character—'*Ni grèves, ni guerre, pour Maigret*'—though he has certainly seen enough of the first and must have taken part in the 1914 holocaust. There are, as he says, far more doctors than politicians in Maigret's chronicles, most of them pale shadows without relief (if the Minister in *Maigret chez le Ministre* is the exception here, this is partly because he is an honest man with the same kind of common background as the Chief-Inspector; the general run are well represented by Charles Besson, the smug baby-kissing, hand-pumping deputy of *Maigret et la Vieille Dame*). Similarly, Maigret's deep feeling for poverty and the poor comes from an understanding of their situation that issues in acceptance rather than in revolt (as with Céline) or in Christian charity (as with Bernanos). Like the poor themselves, Maigret belongs to the silent race. 'The poor,' he reflects, 'are used not to express their hopelessness, because life, work, and the hourly, daily calls of life lie forever ahead of them.' Incidentally, in this connection

[1] Lest this appear churlish, I ought, perhaps, to add that circumstances alter cases. Holmes and Watson (as analysed, for example, in J. A. Holroyd's admirable anthology of exegesis, *Seventeen Steps to 221B*) are the archetypes of a folk-cult that embraces Poirot, Miss Marple, Lord Peter Wimsey, Rex Stout's Nero Wolfe and his assistant Archie, the late Margery Allingham's Albert Campion and a host of others. But what is right for Holmes and the rest is not right for Maigret.

[2] *Op. cit.,* p. 75.

M. de Fallois makes the excellent point that it is part of Maigret's intuition to realize the unsuspected varieties of poverty—the particular fact that it is nowhere more drab than in North Germany or the general truth that, while some things vary from country to country and others remain the same, nothing changes more across the frontiers of Europe than 'the face of misery itself'.

Yet, when all this is said, one cannot entirely agree with M. de Fallois that Maigret is 'apolitical'. True, for him 'not to speak of certain matters is to judge them' and, in this sense, since politicians are concerned primarily with ambition and he, Maigret, is concerned (consumed, rather) with curiosity about human beings, he is wise to leave them alone. Nevertheless, as we shall see, if he is not a politician in the voter's sense, Maigret has his own firm ideas about the social order. One is tempted to call them Confucian. Like most Confucian ideas, they have been implanted in early childhood. Jules Maigret, more than most, is the product of a proper upbringing and a right environment.

His country childhood, its memories and associations, play an immense part in Maigret's make-up, imparting a directness and simplicity to his character, sharpening his awareness of every kind of atmosphere and environment, however stale, however startling. The Chief-Inspector's intuition moves backwards and forwards on two wavelengths: recognition of the familiar and exploration of the unknown. In *Maigret voyage* the journey is not so much Maigret's flight to Switzerland as his voyage of discovery among the very rich in the geography of the Hôtel Georges Cinq. Here the challenge of the unfamiliar is met by Maigret's huge appetite for experience. Assimilation is nine-tenths of the game. When, on the other hand, he ponders the character of Eveline Jave, the murdered young wife of *Maigret s'amuse*, he makes use of his backward wavelength and follows the associations of memory:

> . . . He was picturing again the photograph, the thin thighs, the expression which was lacking in self-confidence, seeming to plead for indulgence and sympathy.
>
> As a small boy, at Paray-le-Frésil, he had felt sorry for rabbits because he thought nature had only created them to serve as food for stronger animals.

Eveline reminded him of the rabbits. She was defenceless. When, as a girl, she used to wander along the beach at Beuzec, couldn't she have been picked up by any man, provided only he showed her a little consideration and tenderness?

Maigret's delight in all kinds of weather—snow, thick fog, sea mist, spring mornings in Paris, fierce heat on the Côte d'Azur and, above all, rain—is part of his childlike pleasure in stopping and staring, following his nose, savouring the moment. (Rain, it has been remarked, plays the same part in the early Maigrets as light played in the work of the Impressionists.) Sitting at the window of his flat in the Boulevard Richard-Lenoir, tranquilly smoking a pipe and watching the lorries coming and going in the warehouse opposite, he experiences 'a sensation which took him back to certain days of his childhood, when his mother was still alive and he was not going to school, because of a cold, or because term had ended. The sensation, in a way, of discovering "what went on when he wasn't there" . . . he was beginning to notice, again, certain tricks of the light, the advance on the pavement of the line between shadow and sunlight, the way things are distorted in the quivering atmosphere of a hot day'. Significantly, Maigret is never more at ease, or more himself, than when he is questioning children (*L'Affaire Saint-Fiacre*, *Le Témoignage de l'Enfant de Choeur*). His general approach to human-beings, what M. de Fallois terms with great exactness 'the mixture of timidity and irony' with which he observes the characters in his cases, is all part of his determination to understand rather than to judge. It is Maigret's disposition to regard so many of his guilty men and women merely as *gamins* and *gamines* that moves him, in *Le Pendu de Saint-Pholien*, to his strange and general act of pardon:

> The four men were walking in step. A breeze had sprung up, and it kept the clouds moving, so that from time to time there was bright moonlight.
> Had they any idea where they were going?
> . . . 'I'm expected in Paris,' Maigret said, stopping suddenly.
> As the three of them looked at him, not knowing whether to feel happy or desperate, and not daring to speak, he stuffed his hands into his pockets.
> 'There are five kids involved . . .'

They were not even sure if they had heard him, because the Inspector had muttered the words to himself between his teeth. Now they could see only his broad back and his black overcoat with the velvet collar receding into the distance . . .

'What were they?' asks Lucas, back at the Quai. 'Anarchists? Forgers? A gang of international crooks?' 'Kids,' he murmured.

Real, positive and, as it were, schematic evil is a much rarer phenomenon in Maigret's epic than in the ordinary type of *roman policier*. Confronted by it, the Inspector is as implacable as any hanging judge. For the gentle silvery old 'marquise' of Etretat (*Maigret et la Vieille Dame*), the odious Mme. Le Cloaguen (*Signé Picpus*) and the rapacious Mme. Serre (*Maigret et la Grande Perche*) there is no pity, only justice. The effort to understand the crime (*comprendre*) is sufficient and no imaginative attempt to put oneself in the criminal's place (*connaître*) is necessary. Vile motives (greed, in all three cases) speak for themselves. To see Maigret *furens* at his most terrible, one must read *Maigret à New York*—and particularly that long spine-chilling confrontation across the Atlantic telephone that concludes the case. Characteristically, it is a true bill made against a crapulous individual whom the law, alas, cannot touch. Again, in a different sense, the reader is often left with the sad knowledge that the real moral culprit of a Maigret drama has gone unscathed. Thus, it is the inhuman Professor Gouin, rather than his crazed and jealous wife, who, in a psychological sense, is the real murderer of Louise Filon (*Maigret se trompe*). Similarly, in *Les Scrupules de Maigret*, even while his interrogation nails the crime of poisoning her brother-in-law squarely on poor Jenny, Maigret finds himself wishing that her cold-hearted sister Gisèle was the guilty party.

'You know my methods, Watson.' Maigret's strength is that he has no method at all. Just as Le Grand Bob's logic of feeling defies all the firm Cartesian principles of his father and his family tradition, so in Maigret's approach to the human mysteries confronting him, 'the intelligence loses its rights', swallowed up in his intuitive effort to put himself in the place of everyone concerned. Each case is less a problem to resolve than a drama to be understood, with Maigret himself playing each part in what Desmond MacCarthy once called 'the theatre under my hat':

He was somewhere far away from the little bar. His wife knew this frame of mind well, as did his colleagues. At the Quai des Orfèvres, when it came over him, people would walk on tip-toe and speak in low voices, for at such times he was capable of flying into a rage as violent as it would be brief, which he would afterwards be the first to regret.

Madame Maigret pushed caution so far as not to look his way and was pretending to skim over the woman's page of the paper, though never ceasing to be alert for her husband's reactions.

He himself would probably not have been able to say what he was thinking about. Perhaps because he wasn't thinking? For it wasn't a question of reasoning. It was rather as if the three characters in the drama had come to life inside him, and even the supers such as Josépha, Antoinette, the young fiancée and Mademoiselle Jusserand, were no longer mere entities but were becoming human beings.

Alas, they were still incomplete, sketchy humans. They remained in a half-light, from which the chief-inspector was striving to drag them with an almost painful effort.

He could feel the truth quite close at hand and he was powerless to grasp it.

The classic description of Maigret's non-method occurs in *Maigret et la Vieille Dame* at the point where Castaing, his local colleague, is discouraged at seeing the Chief-Inspector so drowsy and undecided. As for Maigret himself,

He knew there was a moment like this to get through in every case and that, as if by chance—or was it some sort of instinct which led him?—nearly every time he would have a little too much to drink.

It was when, as he said to himself, it all 'began to rumble'.

At the beginning, he didn't know anything, except precise facts, such as are written in the reports. Then he would find himself among people he had never seen, people he had not known the day before, and he would look at them as one looks at photographs in an album.

He had to get to know them as quickly as possible, to ask questions, believe the answers or not believe them, avoid assuming an opinion too early.

It was the period when people and things were clean-cut but a little distant, still anonymous, impersonal.

Then at a given moment, apparently without any reason, it all 'began to rumble'. The people concerned became at the same time vaguer and more human, in particular they became more complicated, and he had to be careful.

In short, he was beginning to see them from the inside, groping, not sure of himself, with the feeling that it would only need another tiny effort for everything to be clear and for the truth to be revealed by itself.

That 'rumbling' can begin anywhere for Maigret, though ideally he prefers to soak himself in the atmosphere and setting of the case itself: in Jaja's timeless Liberty Bar where the murdered William Brown spent so many happy lost hours of his life and where Maigret 'who had only been there one hour, felt he had known it always'; in the Vernouxs' vast provincial drawing-room with its great crystal chandelier and 'enough armchairs . . . grouped in different corners, and around the fireplace to seat forty people', where the Chief-Inspector, studying the bridge-players, first begins to 'rumble' the suspect in observing his card-play; or in the stable of the *Providence* barge where, at the end of his strangest adventure, Maigret talks on to the dying Darchambaux, 'wondering which he had in front of him at that moment, the sometime doctor, the stubborn convict, the besotted carter, or the infuriated murderer of Mary Lampson'. Yet Maigret's fierce, meditative imagination has no need of time and place. In *Le Fou de Bergerac*, he solves the mystery from his hotel sick-bed; in *Maigret s'amuse* he discovers the murderer merely by analysing the newspapers.

With all this, Maigret is no prodigy, no Sherlock Holmes, let alone his brother Mycroft. In his private capacity, his psychological need to go beyond the line of duty (*La Première Enquête de Maigret*, *Maigret et la Grande Perche*), his low resistance in face of a human mystery, he is very much a hero of our time. If, as M. de Fallois thinks, the essence of heroism is the ability to get mixed up with what does not concern you, Maigret is heroic. (Fittingly, his favourite reading, when confined to the house with one of his frequent colds, are the novels of Dumas.) Yet he remains *un fonctionnaire*, that is to say, a man of limitations, dependent on the hierarchy of his profession and its adjuncts, his superiors at the Quai, the examining magistrates of the Parquet (the odious Coméliau, the sarcastic Amadieu, the agreeable Urbain de Chezaud, the sympathetic Ancelin) and his own devoted squad of inspectors. The last have been depicted so deftly over the years that each of them has long ago taken on a distinct identity of his own and now forms a firm part of the Maigretian legend. There is Lucas, senior of the Chief-Inspector's henchmen, the one with 'the greatest flair and judgment' whose only fault is that 'it was so easy to guess his profession'; there is Janvier, faithful and uxurious, the burly Torrence, and young Lapointe who, with less training and experience than the others, can often pass for a student or a young clerk:

> If he had realized, before setting out that morning, that he was going to have to deal with a tough old maid, he would have brought along young Lapointe rather than Janvier, because, of all the inspectors at Police Headquarters, it was Lapointe who had the greatest success with middle-aged women. One had actually said to him, shaking her head sadly: 'I wonder how a well-bred young man like you can carry on this profession!'
> She had added: 'I'm sure it must go against the grain!'

Lapointe, as befits a tyro, is certainly '*empressé*' with his chief, but it seems rather unfair to describe him, as M. de Fallois does, as '*maladroit*'. On the fringe of Maigret's *clientia* there is the melancholy, tireless, henpecked and generally unfortunate Inspector Lognon (hero of *Maigret et le Fantôme*) and Sergeant Boissier, the safe-breaking expert, a genial but touchy Provençal, his head hardened by countless Pernods. Nor should we forget Dr. Paul, the police surgeon, Moers the ballistics expert or the phlegmatic Chief-Inspector Pyke of Scotland Yard, the most successful of Simenon's imagined Englishmen. All these professional colleagues, whether allies or enemies, fence Maigret in, curbing his imagination, limiting his absorbent nature, blanketing his rage to understand, willing him to see with other eyes.

Even more limiting than his colleagues is the nature of the *métier* itself. Since this is Maigret's chief grievance against his profession, one must be excused for giving it in full, as it occurs in *Maigret aux Assises* where he discusses it with his old friend and physician Dr. Pardon, the G.P.:

> Once, when his surgery had been full all day, Pardon had displayed a touch of discouragement, almost of bitterness.
> 'Twenty-eight patients in the afternoon alone! Hardly time to let them sit down, ask them a few questions. What is it you feel? Where does it hurt? How long has it been going on? The others are

waiting, staring at the padded door, and wondering if their turn will ever come. Show me your tongue! Take off your clothes! In most cases an hour wouldn't be sufficient to find out everything one should know. Each patient is a separate case, and yet I have to work on the conveyor-belt system . . .'

Maigret had then told him of the end-result of his own work, in other words the Assize Court, since most investigations anyway come to their conclusion there.

'Historians,' he had remarked, 'scholars, devote their entire lives to the study of some figure of the past on whom there already exist numerous works. They go from library to library, from archives to archives, search for the least item of correspondence in the hope of grasping a little more of the truth . . .

'For fifty years or more they've been studying Stendhal's letters to get a clearer idea of his character . . .

'Isn't a crime almost always committed by someone out of the ordinary, in other words less easy to comprehend than the man in the street? They give me a few weeks, sometimes only a few days, to steep myself in a new atmosphere, to question ten, twenty, fifty people I knew nothing at all about till then, and, if possible, to sift out the true from the false.

'I've been reproached for going myself onto the scene instead of sending my detectives. You wouldn't believe it, but it's a miracle that I'm still allowed this privilege!

'The examining magistrate, following on from me, had hardly any more scope and he only sees people, detached from their private lives, in the neutral atmosphere of his office.

'All he has in front of him, in fact, are men already reduced to mere diagrams.

'He also has only a limited time at his disposal; hounded by the press, by public opinion, his initiative restricted by a maze of regulations, submerged by administrative formalities which occupy most of his time, what is he likely to find out?

'If it is mere disincarnate beings who leave his office, what is left for the Assizes, and on what basis are the jury going to decide the fate of one or more of their own kindred?'

Dr. Pardon is an intimate part of the Maigret case-book. It is Pardon who warns Maigret against drinking *apéritifs* (a warning that is scantly heeded), Pardon who shows the Chief-Inspector an article in the *Lancet* in which the writer argues that a psychiatrist, if he allows himself to be influenced by theories, will understand his fellow human-beings 'less perfectly than a good schoolmaster, a novelist, or a detective'. Instead of comforting

Maigret, the article has the opposite effect of ruffling him—why, he asks himself indignantly, should the novelist precede the detective? Yet in one sense, as several of his admirers have pointed out, the whole history of Maigret's professional career can be said to have been a prolonged inner transformation from being a simple policeman to becoming a novelist of character *manqué*.

What else do we know of Maigret? That he enjoys his wife's cooking (her *fricandeaux* and *morue à la crème*, her broths and *crème au citron* when he is an invalid), and that, after more than a quarter of a century, he is still discovering unknown sides to Mme. Maigret's character (*Maigret et la Jeune Morte*); that he distrusts psychiatric textbooks, modern methods of detection and 'the evidence of people who have heard something from their beds, perhaps because of my wife'; that he dislikes sleeping in other people's houses and belongs to the generation of men 'many of whom never wanted to drive' ('he personally feared his absent-mindedness, the brown studies he would fall into during an investigation').

The Maigrets' deep personal sadness is the fact that they have never had children. This explains Maigret's sympathy with youth and his understanding of the miseries and falsities, sometimes tragic, sometimes absurd, that trouble the young. Time and again (*Le Revolver de Maigret* and *Maigret en meublé* are the best examples) the action turns on the afflictions of adolescence. Maigret's role as a genuine and particular 'mender of destinies' occurs as far back as *Le Chien Jaune* (1931) where he goes out of his way to set Léon and Emma, young lovers crossed by horrific circumstances, on their proper road.

As for Maigret's basic attitude towards society, I have termed it Confucian, in respectful disagreement here with M. de Fallois who describes the Chief-Inspector as '*un anarchiste foncier*', citing *L'Affaire Saint-Fiacre* as proof of Maigret's final disillusion with the upheld world of his childhood. According to Fallois, it is this '*mythe disparu*' which, despite his long experience of evil, degradation and brutality, has sustained Maigret in his optimism about human-beings. In the *Affaire*, Maigret returns to his native village after thirty years to find the hierarchic, ordered world of innocence that he once knew in sad disarray:

He did not feel like returning to the château. Something there distressed him, made him indignant even.

Admittedly he had no illusions about humanity. But he was furious that his childhood memories should have been sullied. The Countess, above all, whom he had always seen as a noble, beautiful person like a picture-book heroine . . .

And now she had turned out to be a crazy old woman who kept a succession of gigolos.

Not even that. It wasn't frank and open. The notorious Jean pretended to be her secretary. He was not handsome and not very young either.

And the poor old woman, as her son said, was torn between the château and the church.

And the last Comte de Saint-Fiacre was going to be arrested for signing a bad cheque.

The dénouement that follows is one of the best and most memorable in the whole Maigret series, though for once the Chief-Inspector himself is not its precipitant. The crime is solved and the Saint-Fiacre honour avenged by the Count himself who from being a Don Juanish wencher, playboy and passer of bad cheques, takes on a terrible Statue-of-the-Commander accuser's and judge's role at the finish. ('Was the Chief-Inspector mistaken? It seemed to him that Maurice de Saint-Fiacre's lips were touched by the ghost of a smile. Not the smile of a sceptical Parisian, the penniless prodigal. A serene, confident smile . . .')

In *Maigret et les Vieillards* the wheel of the Chief-Inspector's social imagination comes full circle. Entrusted with the case of the murdered ex-ambassador, Maigret at first feels himself quite out of his depth. The motives, thoughts and actions of everyone concerned in the affair are totally at variance with the world of crime that he has spent his life investigating. In his earlier adventures Maigret was concerned largely with the criminal classes—men like Dédé and Arsène (*La Première Enquête de Maigret*) or Pietr-le-Letton's brother or the brutal Picardy gang of *Maigret et son mort*. Later, his cases have grown more domestic, more concerned with the desperate passions of ordinary men and women—bargees and businessmen, milliners and shopkeepers:

> Every time he bought a suit, an overcoat or a pair of shoes, Maigret wore them first of all in the evening, to go for a stroll with his wife through the streets of the district or else to go to the cinema.

'I need to get used to them,' he would say to Madame Maigret when she teased him affectionately.

It was the same when he was immersing himself in a new case. Other people did not realize this, on account of his massive silhouette and the calm expression on his face which they took for self-assurance. In fact, he was going through a more or less prolonged period of hesitation, uneasiness, even timidity.

He had to get used to an unfamiliar setting, to a house, to a way of life, to people who had their own particular habits, their own way of thinking and expressing themselves.

With certain categories of human beings it was relatively easy, for instance with his more or less regular customers or with people like them.

With others he had to start from scratch every time, especially as he distrusted rules and ready-made ideas.

In this new case, he was labouring under an additional handicap. He had made contact, that morning, with a world which was not only very exclusive, but which for him, on account of his childhood, was situated on a very special level . . . this was the effect of a distant period of Maigret's past, the years spent in the shadow of a château of which his father had been the steward and where, for a long time, the Comte and Comtesse de Saint-Fiacre had been, in his eyes, creatures of another species.

The late Comte de Saint-Hilaire's circle confronts Maigret with a Proustian situation which Proust himself would scarcely credit. As he and Janvier scan the Princesse de V-'s amazing letters to the dead man—the day-to-day record of a platonic love affair that has lasted for almost half a century—Maigret, mopping his forehead, is prey to exasperatedly mixed emotions:

. . . They were both of them accustomed to a somewhat crude reality, and the passions with which they came in contact usually took a dramatic turn seeing that they ended up at the Quai des Orfèvres.

Here, on the other hand, it was as difficult as trying to catch hold of a cloud. And when they attempted to grasp the characters, the latter remained as nebulous and unsubstantial as the lady of the lake.

For two pins Maigret would have stuffed all these letters into the green-curtained bookcase, muttering as he did so: 'A lot of rubbish!'

At the same time, he was filled with a certain respect which bordered on emotion. Not wanting to be taken in, he tried to harden his heart.

'Do you believe it all?'

Yet, paradoxically, this is the most personal of all Maigret's cases. In the course of it, his whole lost world of values, shattered in the Saint-Fiacre affair, is restored in its full integrity.

> If he hadn't a very high opinion of men and their capabilities, he went on believing in man himself.
>
> He looked for his weak points. And when, in the end, he put his finger on them, he didn't crow with joy, but on the contrary felt a certain sadness.
>
> Since the previous day, he had felt out of his depth, for he had found himself unexpectedly faced with people whose very existence he had never suspected. All their attitudes, their remarks, their reactions were unfamiliar to him, and he tried in vain to classify them.
>
> He wanted to like them, even Jaquette, for all that she got his back up.
>
> He discovered, in their way of life, a grace, a harmony, a certain innocence too which appealed to him.
>
> Suddenly, he coldly reminded himself: 'Saint-Hilaire has been killed for all that.'

But here Maigret is mistaken. In fact, out of false but entirely honourable motives, the Count has killed himself. It is appropriate that the solution, when it comes, is made by means of an open confession to a priest (the contributor to the *Lancet* was wrong after all!). In this case at least, no one has behaved badly. Maigret's belief in man has, for once, been triumphantly vindicated. No wonder he returns home to Madame Maigret that evening more serious than usual:

> . . . serious and serene, but she did not dare to ask him any questions when, as he kissed her, he pressed her against him for a long time without saying anything.
>
> She could not know that he had just been immersed in a distant past and a rather less distant future.

A fitting note on which to take leave of the observer and mender of destinies.

Chapter 9

BREAKTHROUGH AND BEYOND

IN the course of *Le Grand Bob*, Coindreau, the narrator, finds himself pondering a bitter maxim of Stendhal's to the effect that '*L'homme s'accoûtume à tout excepté au bonheur et au repos*'. Except in Maigret's domestic moments, neither happiness nor repose can be said to have been the keynotes of Simenon's fiction, as he himself has been the first to admit. 'With each successive novel for at least twenty years,' he has written:

> I have been trying to externalize a certain optimism that is in me, a *joie de vivre*, a delight in the immediate and simple communion with all that surrounds me, and to attain, in order to describe such a state, to some kind of serenity. However, after the first third or half, my earlier novels invariably turned into tragedy. For the first time, I was able to create, in *The Little Saint*, a perfectly serene character in immediate contact with nature and life.

Simenon was right to exclaim after writing this book that 'At last I've done it!' *Le Petit Saint* (1965) may not be the greatest of his novels but it is a wonderful study of childhood and an unforgettable picture of working-class poverty in the Paris of the Belle Epoque. Poverty in all its dignity, its acceptance of the things that are, its huge response to the *multum in parvo* of life—the small delights that loom so large in the lives of those with small resources. When the book begins in the early Eighteen-Nineties, Petit-Louis, the Little Saint himself, is between four and five years old. His eldest brother, Vladimir, is about eleven and a half, Alice nine, Guy and Olivier, the red-haired twins, about seven and Emilie six months old. Different fathers have sired them, for their mother Gabrielle, a fruit and vegetable pushcart seller in Montparnasse, is promiscuous but not vicious, a good mother in her slapdash way, hard-working, warm-hearted, the strongest, most strident of life-lovers.

168

Gabrielle, her family and their home, as the small boy sees them, are realized with the blurred reality of a Sickert:

> What mattered most, at first, was the two rooms in which they lived, more exactly the bedroom and the kitchen. During the day, the sheet which hung from copper curtain-rings was pulled back, revealing, on the left side of the window, a very high walnut bed, its two mattresses, its coverlet and the huge quilt.
>
> . . . The walls of the room had formerly been papered, but all that remained was patches on which there were still pictures of persons dressed as in the time of the kings. On one of the patches, near the door, was a young woman with very wide skirts who was on a swing. The rest of the wall was dirty, yellowish plaster on which were initials that had been carved with a knife and pictures representing genital organs which someone had tried to rub out. Who had drawn them? Who had tried to efface them?
>
> Not his mother, in all likelihood. When the weather was warm, it didn't bother her in the least to walk around naked in the room and even in the kitchen. When she had not yet put up her big red bun, her hair hung down to her waist, and the bush at the bottom of her slightly plump belly was very fine and fluffy, of the same light shade as Alice's hair.
>
> She was cheerful and often sang while doing the housework, when she had time to do it.
>
> . . . His mother laughed as often as she sang. When she was in bed with a man she began by sighing and moaning, but it always ended with a burst of laughter.

As the book proceeds and the traits of the Heurteau family pile up, the children's characters emerge with brutal clarity. Vladimir is a tough and, as events turn out, a thief and a drug-peddler. Alice, pale but pretty, is a proven slut set early on her path by having sex with her eldest brother. 'There was a feeling in the air that things were starting to go to pieces . . . one shitting business as Gabrielle, with her fondness for expressive words, used to say, brings another.' The twins take to skipping school, become tearaways and eventually decamp with the family savings. They are retrieved by the police, but eventually leave home for good. All the while the position of each member of the family in the Rue Mouffetard is shifting in time, changing with the years, so that 'Vladimir had suddenly become a man whom his mother asked for advice, whereas Alice remained a girl for a while and the

difference of age between her and the twins and then between her
and Louis mattered less and less'.

Meanwhile the Little Saint himself has been growing up. The
nickname has been given him at school, not because he is
religious-minded or even particularly good (as his mother
scathingly remarks, 'Religion is for the rich!') but simply because
he always manages to stay out of trouble. It will stick with him
all his life. From the first the reader realizes that Petit-Louis is
somehow set apart from the others—a day-dreamer, not talking
much, preferring to look and smell and touch, observing everything
around him with a mysterious delight, from the rumblings of the
family stove to his mother's gentlemen callers, especially the loud
and hilarious M. Pliska. Above all, he loves the market life of Les
Halles where he accompanies Gabrielle in the early mornings.
Time flows on in the street, Petit-Louis leaves school and takes
a job as a clerk in the market; the war leaves few traces on either,
since he is too short-statured to be called up and the Rue
Mouffetard 'was a street in which people's main concern was to
get enough food every day, and, for those who had children,
to feed them'. When Petit-Louis buys his first tube of paint
at a stationer's, the casually kept secret of his destiny is at last
revealed.

The final forty pages of the novel telescope the Little Saint's life
through the years that follow. At the end we are left with a strange
old man who walks with short steps, conscious of his fragility,
who has kept a green heart and knows that he still has much
to do:

> He had worked a great deal. He was still working. It would take
> him years more to render what he felt had always been in him.
> 'What exactly is your aim?'
> 'I don't know.'
> That was the sentence that he had uttered most often in the
> course of his life and which he kept repeating.
> Monsieur Suard was dead. His son, who had taken over the
> gallery, called him Maître. Many people called him Maître.
> He remembered the evening when he had thought he saw a slight
> cloud come over his mother's face, which had always been radiant.
> One of the twins was dead. Emilie was dead. Pretty Alice was fat
> and callous. She too was clouded over. And Vladimir had no chance

of getting out of prison alive. Only one of them was left, far away, in Ecuador, and he had stopped writing. He was nearing seventy-five and his wife was over eighty. Were they still alive and were they still hunting for butterflies and birds of paradise?

At times he thought he could feel the cloud coming over him too. He would think of the mattresses, of Emilie's cot, of the Rue Mouffetard, of the push-carts arriving at Les Halles.

Had he not taken something from everything and everyone? Had he not used their substance?

He didn't know, he mustn't know, otherwise he would be unable to carry on to the end.

A novel of sentiment? One must suppose so, though it never declines into the sentimental, for it is too briskly told and too crisply written to permit of such extravagance. As he follows in the wake of Petit-Louis and Gabrielle, making their way across Paris in the dawn with their pushcart, loving life and one another so much, understanding one another so little, the reader is put in mind of the famous couplets that end Baudelaire's *Le Crépuscule du Matin*:

> *L'aurore grelottante en robe rose et verte*
> *S'avançait lentement sur la Seine déserte,*
> *Et le sombre Paris, en se frottant les yeux,*
> *Empoignait ses outils, vieillard laborieux.*

He is also reminded of the sentence that concludes a part of Gargantua's adventures: '*Ainsi ils continuèrent joyeusement leur chemin.*'

Le Confessionnal (1966), coming, as it did, immediately after *Le Petit Saint*, disappoints. It is extraordinary that Simenon who, in his Maigret books, handles adolescents and their problems with such un-heavy-handed understanding, generally only manages to make them unnatural or boring in his other books. Earlier I referred to *Les Soeurs Lacroix*—that travesty of the French family hearth, with its quarter-century feuds and its incredible and ghoulish heroine, Geneviève Vernes, lying in bed and willing herself to die, stark mad, as it were, in white satin. *Le Confessionnal*, by contrast, is an accurate and humdrum piece of domestic *rapportage*. The basic situation, while it probably exists in a hundred thousand French households, is without question sad but it is tedious nonetheless. For once, incredibly, Simenon has contrived to be dull. Otherwise, this tale of a sixteen-year-old being used by his doting parents as the self-justifying receptacle (confessional?) of their antagonisms and alienation, is hard to fault. André Bar himself is a perfectly ordinary *lycée*-milk bar product, his girl friend Francine a wise and understanding teenager. The mother drinks, takes barbiturates and has lovers as, alas, many twentieth-century mothers do. The conclusion, when it comes, is as trite and as foreseeable as any end-dialogue heard in the French theatre during the last thirty years or more:

> 'At such times she's ashamed of herself, and horribly unhappy. She saw you in a street in Nice, when she was coming out of a *maison de rendez-vous*.'
> 'Was it Nival?'
> 'No. A croupier from the casino.'
> His father rose, heavily.
> 'That's all, son. I've persuaded her to stay. She needs your help even more than mine. This evening she's gone to dinner with Natasha to tell her she's going to stop seeing her . . .
> 'She knows that we're by ourselves and that I'm talking to you. Tomorrow she'll be scanning your face for signs of our conversation. I should so like you to show her a little tenderness. Not pity, just tenderness!'
> He walked towards the door with uncertain steps and turned round to say, in a low voice: 'Perhaps you'll be better able to do so than I was. Goodnight, André.'

Goodnight, indeed. The moral of the book would seem to be a variant of Sidney Smith's dictum. It is the child, not the parent, who leads 'the life of a gambler'.

La Mort d'Auguste, published later in the same year as *Le Confessionnal*, is a very different kettle of fish. This is Simenon and Sim at their best, with Sim's genius for telling a story harnessed to Simenon's phenomenal grasp of human nature—a grasp which, in some chemical and inexplicable way, seems only to grow with the years. Few writers in their sixties have displayed such capacity for development.

Ever since Hitler's war ended, Auguste Mature's 'Chez L'Auvergnat' (founded in 1913) has flourished mightily. From a humble *bistro* in the Les Halles neighbourhood, it has become the resort of discriminating gastronomes without ever losing its specialized, highly local flavour. Tonight, with Antoine, old Auguste's son, at his command post, Fernande, Antoine's wife, at the *caisse*, and a large party from the British Embassy singing the cuisine's praises, the wheels of the restaurant are turning with their accustomed rhythm. Outside, the great market is revving away in preparation for the long night ahead, its vast galleries already lighted up. Suddenly Auguste, who has been telling a newly-wedded couple the ancient mariner tale of his success, collapses at their table. He is carried upstairs to his bed and, shortly afterwards, he dies. The subsequent search for his missing will and the mystification involved in the matter is the situation on which the novel turns. So far full marks for Sim's construction. What takes the book out of the class of good mysteries (and, after all, *they* are not as thick on the literary ground as they were fifty years ago) are the characters of Auguste's three sons and their wives and their separate reactions to the large inheritance that seems, tantalizingly, just outside their grasp.

There is Ferdinand the judge, the eldest of the three, the son who escaped early from the bistro and has always turned up his nose at the family business, but to whose life (and the life of his brittle would-be smart wife, Véronique) that share in his father's one million francs will make all the difference. There is Bernard, the youngest son, the out-of-work rotter and black sheep of the family and his long-suffering Nicole. And there is the punctilious, devoted Antoine, who has stuck by his father and the restaurant throughout (much to the others' scorn and to Bernard's envy) and now sees his loyalty rewarded in standing possessed of the only palpable asset that the old man appears to have left— 'Chez l'Auvergnat' itself, which by a previous agreement with his father, it now turns out that he mostly owns.

We have remarked before on Simenon's loathing of the law in both its branches, judge and advocate alike (*'Je déteste cette assurance!'*). In one scene of this novel he neatly kills both birds with a single stone. Back at the Palais de Justice, his father's missing fortune crowding everything else out of his head, Ferdinand forces himself to concentrate on the examination of René Mauvis, the notorious embezzler:

'Has Superintendent Brabant not telephoned?'
'He is on the track of a new witness, sir. He is afraid he won't be able to join you today because of the weekend . . .'
If his share of his father's million was found, should he retire at once? He thought seriously about it while he sharpened his pencil.
No! Even with that, they wouldn't have enough to live on. He'd do better to wait for his retirement age and take the full pension . . .
But, in fact, what would he do with his time, once he retired?
Should they sell their flat, that had cost so dear, and was too big for the two of them already?
And to go where? To the country? Neither he nor Véronique liked the country . . .
He suddenly felt naked, vulnerable. He'd always believed that he had organized a proper life for himself, satisfying, enviable even. Suddenly he realized that he had nothing at the end of it.
Unless, perhaps, they found this missing million, a million which he had not earned, which came from outside, from his father's and mother's patient toil in the bistro he had been so ashamed of, then the old man and Antoine working together . . .
Not that he accused Antoine of cheating. Though no doubt his brother had profited from the business. And he'd taken care to get their father to sign that bit of paper.
Of course, there was no proof that the paper was enough in itself to establish his brother's rights. Ferdinand was seldom concerned with the Civil Code, especially the commercial Section.
He stared, unseeing, at the first typed sheet of the dossier in front of him. He heard someone cough. It was one of the gendarmes who had brought in René Mauvis . . .
'Sit down . . . your counsel isn't here? You're sure you summoned him, Dubois?'

Half an hour later, still weighing his personal pros and cons, he tells his clerk to 'Ring Maître Gerbois's office'—only to learn that the lawyer, quite forgetting his imprisoned client, has gone off with his wife to the country for the week-end. With a wave of the hand, the unfortunate handcuffed Mauvis is dismissed back to the Dépôt, leaving the judge to concentrate on his problems once more.

Balzac might have faintly approved *La Mort d'Auguste*. He would have enthused over *Le Chat* (1967), the chilliest of Simenon's later fantasies. It concerns an old Parisian married couple, he a widower, she a widow, who have, as a result of horrible circumstances connected with the death of their respective pets, silently resolved to live out their lives together in unremitting, creative hatred. How Emile Bouin, ex-mason, surveyor and rough diamond, having lost his jolly, working-class wife, came to court and marry Marguerite Charmois, the frail, genteel relict of the late Frédéric Charmois, sometime first violinist of the Opéra, is a story that only Balzac or Simenon could tell. He tells it inimitably, almost as though, after so many triumphant human tragedies of his own, he had decided to allow himself the luxury of one *Comédie Humaine* excursion. Backwards and forwards the narrative goes, zig-zagging between time past in the couple's separate lives and time present in the silence and enormity of their existence together in the quiet house in the Impasse de Feuillantines, never speaking, addressing one another by written notes which he flicks like darts across the living room and she leaves ostentatiously on the piano. A tour de force of the macabre, told with such a quiet, collected power of imagination that the reader, even while he gapes and shudders, somehow never thinks of asking himself, can such things be?

I think that Balzac would only fault *Le Chat* in one respect— a simple ambiguity, yet one on which the whole plot and structure of the novel must be allowed to turn. Did Bouin's wife poison his cat or not? Certainly he never doubted that she did. It was because he was convinced of this that he himself, in a particularly horrible fashion, destroyed her parrot. Balzac would have cleared this point up at once. Simenon—it is one of the multiple imaginative differences between them—prefers to leave the reader with a disturbing feeling that the case is 'not proven'.

This strain of ambiguity runs all through Simenon's fiction, infuriating or disquieting many of his readers, attracting others by its faithful rendering of those mysteries in life which we have all encountered, at one time or another, in the lives of our fellow human beings. (At a different and socially comic level, it is this element of uncertainty about other people's actions and motives that adds so much to the truth and piquancy of the narrator Jenkins's reminiscences in Anthony Powell's 'Music of Time'

SIMENON IN COURT

series.) A distinguished novelist has told me how she once questioned Simenon about the strange and unaccounted-for death of old Oscar Donadieu, the tyrant dynast of the family. Did he fall into the *bassin*, she asked, or was he pushed? The writer professed not to know. At first one is reminded of Browning's reputed replies to Browning Society questioners. In fact, I am sure that here Simenon was quite simply telling the truth.

In the latest of his novels, *Le Déménagement* (1968), this element of ambiguity lies at the very centre of the book. In a foreword Simenon writes that certain of his critics and foreign publishers, '*habitués aux beaux gros livres, bien gras*', have reproached him for only writing short novels and this one is particularly so; it runs, in the original typescript version, to 127 pages. He adds that although he could easily have spun it out ('worded' it out—*délayé*) to do so would have been to cheat himself and his readers.

In fact, as usual Simenon manages to cram more into this book than most of his fellow-practitioners could contrive to do in three times the space. Briefly, it concerns a certain Emile Jovis, aged thirty-five, the branch head of a travel bureau, who has moved his family (wife and son) out of Paris to a flat in one of the new *cités modernes*—those great blocks of megalithic, somewhat sinister architecture that one sees on the way from the airport at Orly. For Jovis, a worried, conformist, status-ridden executive, a man with the best intentions who loves his family and is anxious to do what he thinks is best for them, the move to 'Clairevie' is a step up the 'rep' ladder of perfection. Blanche, the wife, though hating to be uprooted, gives in, as she always does. Alain, a bright, intelligent schoolboy of thirteen, is, as usual, not afraid to question his father's actions and assumptions. (One of Jovis's domestic crosses is that he and his son are seldom *en rapport*.) Alain's comments throughout the book are a puncturing comment on his father's whole code of life and a joy to the reader. What a name, 'Clairevie'!—not a village, not a hamlet, just '*un terrain vague*' ('*On ne se promène pas dans un terrain vague*'). ' "What will mama do all day?" asked the boy. "What do you mean? What she has always done." "And you believe that?" Suddenly, he didn't believe it at all. That is, not any more . . .'

At night, taking a walk with his father, Alain examines the

cars outside the block of flats. He notes that the bright red sports roadster is missing and remarks: 'That doesn't surprise me. Whoever owns a car like that never gets home early.' The car belongs, as his father knows, to the Farrans, mysterious neighbours from the flat next door, whose bed conversation, part criminal, part obscene, has, through some constructional fault in the masonry, kept poor Jovis tormented, titillated and consumed with avid curiosity for several nights running (Blanche is the soundest of sleepers). Car thefts, unnameable sexual activities and a night club which Farran either owns or manages, form the recurrent theme of these 3 a.m. dialogues. In the upshot, Jovis makes his way to the 'Carillon'—and later meets his death in a mysterious burst of gunfire. Here it is not a question of 'did he fall or was he pushed?' as precisely who killed him and why.

Le Déménagement, like its predecessors, is something more than just another unsolved mystery. It is a book to be read at several levels. Jovis and his son, for example, not only typify a complete change in the nature of child-parent relationship that has occurred among the educated West over the last half century, but they are given sharper focus through the way in which the writer sketches in Jovis's relationship—lack of it, rather—with *his* father, the dour, anti-clerical schoolmaster. Blanche, too, has a tragic background of her own—a background that more than accounts for her complete self-effacement in the line of life. Once more the master is shown not to have lost his cunning.

The author of *Le Déménagement* has never laid claim to his public, historical patch of time in the sense that Sartre recommends. Yet the Little Saint of the Parisian 1890's to the schoolboy-teenager of the *cité moderne*, with all the private worlds that lie between them, represents a remarkable curve of the social imagination. In George Steiner's *Language of Silence* (p. 237), having reflected that 'it is by no means evident that civilization will produce in future those constructs of verbal syntactic representation, or *mimesis*, which we find in Dante, Shakespeare and Joyce', the writer remarks that 'Simenon may be among the last to have taken an entire culture for his verbal canvas'. The attempt to describe something of the size and variety of Simenon's human canvas has been the object of this brief and partial study.

ENVOY

DURING a visit to Liège two years ago, I called upon Mme. Simenon, now in her ninety-second year, and she received me with great kindness. A frail old lady, with piercing pale blue eyes and a dramatic whisper. 'Have you read Georges's latest book,' she said, tapping *La Mort d'Auguste* on a table near her armchair, her voice sinking a shade lower. 'It is about a missing will, monsieur . . .' Just the voice, you felt, that the mother of one of the world's supreme story-tellers should possess.

At any time during the last quarter of a century or more, Mme. Simenon could have lived anywhere in the world that she chose. She has chosen to remain in her apartment in the same neighbourhood as the Rue Puits-en-Sock a few hundred yards away from where Roger Mamelin's grandfather had his hatter's shop and a stone's throw from the Rue Léopold where Mme. Simenon herself kept that boarding-house that has since passed into literature.

Listening to her, you could not describe Georges Simenon's mother as an old lady living in the past, though in Liège she has long been a legendary figure, a celebrity whom the Prefect and the Mayor do themselves the honour of calling ceremoniously upon each year. Casting an eye over the huge folio of cuttings that she showed me, I was amused to find her depicted—in an extract from that same *Gazette de Liège* on which her son once proudly served as an apprentice-reporter—as '*diablement alerte*'. She was not at all unwilling to talk about the days passed long ago in that lost world that is now embalmed in *Pedigree*. Remembering her eldest son as he was in his boyhood, she made two remarks that struck me forcibly—'*Georges aimait toujours les petits-gens*' and '*Georges était très fier*' with its characteristic addition '*mais, voyez vous, monsieur, c'était une fierté très mal placée*'. The two phrases may well serve as an epilogue to this book.

Appendix

BOOKS BY GEORGES SIMENON

Original French title	Title of first English translation	Year of publication in France	Year of publication in England
Pietr-le-Letton	The Strange Case of Peter the Lett (in Inspector Maigret Investigates)	1930	1933
M. Gallet, décédé	The Death of M. Gallet (in Introducing Inspector Maigret)	1931	1933
Le Pendu de Saint-Pholien	The Crime of Inspector Maigret (in Introducing Inspector Maigret)	1931	1933
Le Charretier de 'la Providence'	The Crime at Lock 14 (in The Triumph of Inspector Maigret)	1931	1934
La Tête d'un Homme	A Battle of Nerves (in The Patience of Maigret)	1931	1939
Le Chien Jaune	A Face for a Clue (in The Patience of Maigret)	1931	1939
Un Crime en Hollande	A Crime in Holland (in Maigret Abroad)	1931	1940

Original French title	Title of first English translation	Year of publication in France	Year of publication in England
La Danseuse du Gai Moulin	At the Gai-Moulin (in Maigret Abroad)	1931	1940
La Guingette à deux Sous	The Guingette by the Seine (in Maigret to the Rescue	1931	1940
La Nuit du Carrefour	The Crossroad Murders (in Inspector Maigret Investigates)	1932	1933
Le Port des Brumes	Death of a Harbour-master (in Maigret and M. L'Abbé)	1932	1941
L'Ombre Chinoise	The Shadow on the Court-yard (in The Triumph of Inspector Maigret)	1932	1934
Chez les Flamands	The Flemish Shop (in Maigret to the Rescue)	1932	1940
Le Fou de Bergerac	The Madman of Bergerac (in Maigret Travels South)	1932	1940
Liberty Bar	Liberty Bar (in Maigret Travels South)	1932	1940
Le Passager du 'Polarlys'	The Mystery of the 'Polarlys' (in In Two Latitudes)	1932	1942
Les Treize Coupables		1932	

Original French title	Title of first English translation	Year of publication in France	Year of publication in England
Les Treize Mystères		1932	
Les Treize Énigmes		1932	
Le Relais d'Alsace	The Man from Everywhere (in Maigret and M. L'Abbé)	1933	1941
Au Rendez-vous des Terre-Neuvas	The Sailor's Rendezvous (in Maigret Keeps a Rendez-vous)	1933	1940
L'Affaire Saint-Fiacre	The Saint-Fiacre Affair (in Maigret Keeps a Rendez-vous	1933	1940
L'Écluse No. 1	The Lock at Charenton (in Maigret Sits it Out)	1933	1941
Les Gens d'en Face	The Window Over the Way	1933	1951
L'Âne Rouge		1933	
La Maison du Canal	The House by the Canal	1933	1952
Les Fiancailles de Monsieur Hire	Mr. Hire's Engagement (in The Sacrifice)	1933	1956
Le Coup de Lune	Tropic Moon (in In Two Latitudes)	1933	1942

Original French title	Title of first English translation	Year of publication in France	Year of publication in England
Le Haut Mal	The Woman in the Grey House (in Affairs of Destiny)	1933	1942
Maigret	Maigret Returns (in Maigret Sits it Out)	1934	1941
L'Homme de Londres	Newhaven-Dieppe (in Affairs of Destiny)	1934	1942
Le Locataire	The Lodger (in Escape in Vain)	1934	1943
Les Suicidés	One Way Out (in Escape in Vain)	1934	1943
Les Pitard	A Wife at Sea	1934	1949
Les Clients d'Avrenos		1935	
Quartier Nègre		1935	
L'Évadé	The Disintegration of J.P.G.	1936	1937
Les Demoiselles de Concarneau	The Breton Sisters (in Havoc by Accident)	1936	1943
45° à L'Ombre		1936	
Long Cours		1936	
Faubourg	Home Town (in On the Danger Line)	1937	1944

Original French title	Title of first English translation	Year of publication in France	Year of publication in England
L'Assassin	The Murderer (in A Wife at Sea)	1937	1949
Le Blanc à Lunettes	Havoc by Accident	1937	1943
Le Testament Donadieu	The Shadow Falls	1937	1945
Les Sept Minutes		1938	
Les Rescapés du 'Télémaque'	The Survivors (in Black Rain)	1938	1949
La Mauvaise Étoile		1938	
Chemin Sans Issue	Blind Path (in Lost Moorings)	1938	1946
Touriste de Bananes	Banana Tourist (in Lost Moorings)	1938	1946
L'Homme qui Regardait Passer les Trains	The Man who Watched the Trains Go By	1938	1942
Les Trois Crimes de Mes Amis		1938	
Monsieur La Souris	Monsieur La Souris (in Poisoned Relations)	1938	1950
La Marie du Port	Chit of a Girl	1938	1949

Original French title	Title of first English translation	Year of publication in France	Year of publication in England
Le Suspect	The Green Thermos (in On the Danger Line)	1938	1944
Les Soeurs Lacroix	Poisoned Relations	1938	1950
Le Cheval Blanc		1938	
Ceux de la Soif		1938	
Le Coup de Vague		1939	
Chez Krull	Chez Krull (in A Sense of Guilt)	1939	1955
Le Bourgmestre de Furnes	The Burgomaster of Furnes	1939	1952
Les Inconnus dans la Maison	The Strangers in the House	1940	1951
Malempin		1940	
Cour d'Assises	Justice (in Chit of a Girl)	1941	1949
La Maison des sept Jeunes Filles		1941	
L'Outlaw		1941	
Bergelon		1941	
Il Pleut, Bergère	Black Rain	1941	1949
Le Voyageur de la Toussaint	Strange Inheritance	1941	1950

Original French title	Title of first English translation	Year of publication in France	Year of publication in England
L'Oncle Charles s'est Enfermé		1941	
La Veuve Couderc	Ticket of Leave	1942	1954
Le Fils Cardinaud	Young Cardinaud (in The Sacrifice)	1942	1956
La Vérité sur Bébé Donge	The Trial of Bébé Donge	1942	1952
Maigret Revient		1942	
Le Petit Docteur		1943	
Les Dossiers de L'Agence O		1943	
Les Nouvelles Enquêtes de Maigret		1944	
Signé Picpus	To Any Lengths (in Maigret on Holiday)	1944	1950
Le Rapport du Gendarme	The Gendarme's Report (in The Window Over the Way)	1944	1951
La Fenêtre des Rouet	Across the Street	1945	1954
L'Aîné des Ferchaux	Magnet of Doom	1945	1948

S.I.C.—12*

Original French title	Title of first English translation	Year of publication in France	Year of publication in England
Je me Souviens		1945	
Les Noces de Poitiers		1946	
Le Cercle des Mahé		1946	
La Fuite de Monsieur Monde	Monsieur Monde Vanishes	1946	1967
Trois Chambres à Manhattan		1946	
Au Bout du Rouleau		1947	
Le Clan des Os-tendais	The Ostenders (in The House by the Canal)	1947	1952
Lettre à Mon Juge	Act of Passion	1947	1953
Le Destin des Malou	The Fate of the Malous	1947	1962
La Pipe de Maigret and *Maigret se Fâche*		1947	
Maigret à New York		1947	
Maigret et l'Inspecteur Malchanceux		1947	

Original French title	Title of first English translation	Year of publication in France	Year of publication in England
Pedigree	Pedigree	1948	1962
Le Bilan Malétras		1948	
Le Passager Clandestin	The Stowaway	1948	1957
La Jument Perdue		1948	
La Neige était sale	The Stain on the Snow	1948	1953
Les Vacances de Maigret	Maigret on Holiday	1948	1950
Maigret et Son Mort	Maigret's Special Murder	1948	1964
Le Fond de la Bouteille		1949	
Les Fantômes du Chapelier	The Hatter's Ghosts (in The Judge and the Hatter)	1949	1956
Les Quatre Jours du Pauvre Homme		1949	
Mon Ami Maigret	My Friend Maigret	1949	1956
Maigret Chez le Coroner		1949	
Un Nouveau dans la Ville		1950	

Original French title	Title of first English translation	Year of publication in France	Year of publication in England
Les Volets Verts	The Heart of a Man (in A Sense of Guilt)	1950	1955
L'Enterrement de Monsieur Bouvet	Inquest on Bouvet	1950	1958
Tante Jeanne	Aunt Jeanne	1950	1953
Maigret et les Petits Cochons sans Queue		1950	
L'Amie de Madame Maigret	Madame Maigret's Friend	1950	1960
Les Mémoires de Maigret	Maigret's Memoirs	1950	1963
Le Temps d'Anaïs		1951	
Une Vie comme neuve	A New Lease of Life	1951	1963
Marie qui Louche		1951	
La Première Enquête de Maigret	Maigret's First Case	1951	1958
Maigret et la Vieille Dame	Maigret and the Old Lady	1951	1958
Un Noël de Maigret		1951	

Original French title	Title of first English translation	Year of publication in France	Year of publication in England
Maigret au 'Picratt's'	Maigret in Montmartre (in Maigret Right and Wrong)	1951	1954
Maigret en Meublé	Maigret Takes a Room	1951	1960
Maigret et la Grande Perche	Maigret and the Burglar's Wife	1951	1955
La Mort de Belle	Belle (in Violent Ends)	1952	1954
Les Frères Rico	The Brothers Rico (in Violent Ends)	1952	1954
Maigret, Lognon et les Gangsters		1952	
Le Revolver de Maigret	Maigret's Revolver	1952	1956
Antoine et Julie		1953	
L'Escalier de Fer	The Iron Staircase	1953	1963
Feux Rouges	Red Lights (in Danger Ahead)	1953	1955
Maigret et l'Homme du Banc		1953	
Maigret a Peur	Maigret Afraid	1953	1961
Maigret se Trompe	Maigret's Mistake (in Maigret Right and Wrong)	1953	1954

Original French title	Title of first English translation	Year of publication in France	Year of publication in England
Le Bateau d'Émile		1954	
Crime Impuni	Account Unsettled	1954	1962
L'Horloger d'Everton	The Watchmaker of Everton (in Danger Ahead)	1954	1955
Le Grand Bob		1954	
Maigret à l'École	Maigret Goes to School	1954	1957
Maigret et la Jeune Morte	Maigret and the Young Girl	1954	1955
Maigret chez le Ministre		1954	
Les Témoins	The Witnesses (in The Judge and the Hatter)	1955	1956
La Boule Noire		1955	
Les Complices	The Accomplices	1955	1966
Maigret Tend un Piège	Maigret Sets a Trap	1955	1965
Maigret et le Corps sans Tête	Maigret and the Headless Corpse	1955	1967
En Cas de Malheur	In Case of Emergency	1956	1960
Le Petit Homme d'Arkhangelsk	The Little Man from Archangel	1956	1957

Original French title	Title of first English translation	Year of publication in France	Year of publication in England
Un Échec de Maigret	Maigret's Failure	1956	1962
Le Fils	The Son	1957	1958
Le Nègre	The Negro	1957	1959
Maigret s'amuse	Maigret's Little Joke	1957	1957
Strip-Tease	Striptease	1958	1959
Le Président	The Premier	1958	1961
Le Passage de la Ligne		1958	
Maigret Voyage		1958	
Les Scruples de Maigret	Maigret Has Scruples	1958	1959
Dimanche	Sunday	1959	1960
La Vieille		1959	
Le Veuf	The Widower	1959	1961
Maigret et les Témoins Recalcitrants	Maigret and the Reluctant Witnesses	1959	1959
Une Confidence de Maigret	Maigret Has Doubts	1959	1968
L'Ours en Peluche		1960	

Original French title	Title of first English translation	Year of publication in France	Year of publication in England
Maigret aux Assises	Maigret in Court	1960	1961
Maigret et les Vieillards	Maigret in Society	1960	1962
Betty		1961	
Le Train	The Train	1961	1964
Maigret et le Voleur Paresseux	Maigret and the Lazy Burglar	1961	1963
La Porte	The Door	1962	1964
Les Autres		1962	
Maigret et les Braves Gens		1962	
Maigret et le Client du Samedi	Maigret and the Saturday Caller	1962	1964
La Colère de Maigret	Maigret Loses His Temper	1962	1965
Les Anneaux de Bicêtre	The Patient	1963	1963
Maigret et le Clochard		1963	
La Rue aux Trois Poussins		1964	

Original French title	Title of first English translation	Year of publication in France	Year of publication in England
La Chambre Bleue	The Blue Room	1964	1965
L'Homme au Petit Chien	The Man with the Little Dog	1964	1965
Maigret et le Fantôme		1964	
Maigret se défend	Maigret on the Defensive	1964	1966
Le Petit Saint	The Little Saint	1965	1966
Le Train de Venise		1965	
La Patience de Maigret	The Patience of Maigret	1965	1966
Le Confessionnal	The Confessional	1966	1967
La Mort d'Auguste	The Old Man Dies	1966	1968
Maigret et l'Affaire Nahour	Maigret and the Nahour Case	1967	1967
Le Voleur de Maigret	Maigret's Pickpocket	1967	1968
Le Chat		1967	
Le Déménagement	The Neighbours	1967	1968
Maigret à Vichy		1968	
La Prison		1968	